HOW TO PASS

TECHNICAL SELECTION TESTS

D0589302

For my daughter Simrun – Sanjay Modha
and Ella Schlesinger – Mike Bryon

HOW TO PASS

TECHNICAL SELECTION TESTS

2ND EDITION

Mike Bryon & Sanjay Modha

KOGAN
PAGE

Publisher's note
Every possible effort has been made to ensure that the information contained in this book is accurate at the time of going to press, and the publishers and authors cannot accept responsibility for any errors or omissions, however caused. No responsibility for loss or damage occasioned to any person acting, or refraining from action, as a result of the material in this publication can be accepted by the editor, the publisher or any of the authors.

First published in 1993, entitled *Technical Selection Tests and How to Pass Them*
Reprinted in 1994, entitled *How to Pass Technical Selection Tests*
Reprinted 1995, 1997 (twice), 1998, 2000, 2002
Second edition 2005

120 Pentonville Road
London N1 9JN
United Kingdom
www.kogan-page.co.uk

British Library Cataloguing-in-Publication Data

A CIP record for this book is available from the British Library.

ISBN 0 7494 4375 8

Typeset by Saxon Graphics Ltd, Derby
Printed and bound in Great Britain by Creative Print and Design (Wales), Ebbw Vale

Contents

Introduction

The use of selection tests in the recruitment and selection of candidates has seen a huge increase over the last several years. These tests are also widely used in the selection process for many vocational courses and also for modern apprenticeships.

For many large employers, the use of selection tests forms an integral part of their selection process. There are many benefits for the employer. The use of technical selection tests is a very useful and cost-effective way of identifying people with a technical aptitude. The recruitment, selection and training of an employee is a costly affair, in both time and money. Thus employers use these tests to eliminate people at the first stage. However, many candidates who may have the aptitude for the job fail to get selected because they are unaware of the test demands, and are generally unprepared and not test-wise.

The aim of this book is to help people to prepare for the technical selection tests. The book contains hundreds of typical questions found in the selection tests. Lots of practice is essential if you are to show your full potential in a selection test, and this is why this book is so valuable.

If you are applying for work, a course or an apprenticeship in industries such as building and construction, electrical, electronic or mechanical engineering and many other trades, then you will find it essential preparation. The book contains an essential dictionary of technical terms, and hundreds of practice questions that cover verbal, numerical and diagrammatic reasoning.

The Kogan Page testing series includes titles aimed at all levels and most areas of testing. This book is the ideal starting point for a candidate facing tests at the intermediate level.

The idea for this book arose from our work in pre-employment training for some of the largest employers in the UK. Our work involved preparing people for the selection process of these organisations and the posts that they would go on to fill. This experience led us to conclude that many people who fail the tests could in fact pass them. What is required is that they come to terms with their anxieties and prepare prior to the test. The purpose of this book is to make available to a general readership the strategies developed while preparing candidates for the selection tests.

Since its publication, *How to Pass Technical Selection Tests* has been translated and published in Portugal and Spain. It has been of considerable help to thousands of people who face employers' tests. This second edition ensures that the practice material continues to help candidates prepare for the challenge of selection tests.

We have endeavoured to ensure that there are no errors in this book. However, if you find any then please accept our apologies and be kind enough to inform us of them so that they can be removed from the next reprint.

A brief guide to tests

What are selection tests?

Tests have been used for many years now and are quite commonly referred to as selection tests. Selection tests, as the name suggests, are tests that are designed and used for the purpose of selecting and allocating people. The tests can be used in a number of situations, for example in selecting for jobs, in promoting or transferring people to other departments, and in certain types of course and career counselling. These tests are known as psychometric tests, also sometimes called psychological tests.

Psychometric tests are one way of establishing or confirming an applicant's competence for the job. They can be useful provided they are *reliable* and *valid* for the job for which they are being used. Selection tests are standardised sets of questions or problems that allow an applicant's performance to be compared with that of other people of a similar background. For example, if you are a graduate your score would be compared to the scores of other graduates, or if you have few or no qualifications your score would be compared to people who are similar to you, and so on. What this means is that the tests are norm referenced (the section 'Test scores' below explains what is meant by 'norm referenced').

Do tests discriminate?

All good tests discriminate! That, after all, is the purpose of the test. However, this discrimination should be on the basis of ability. This is fair and legal discrimination.

If the tests, or the way in which they are used, discriminate on the basis of sex or race then this is unfair and possibly even illegal under the Sex Discrimination Act or the Race Relations Act. It does not matter whether the unfair discrimination is intentional or unintentional. However, the Acts do not explicitly refer to testing. The implication of the two Acts is that, if the use of the tests (or other selection methods) results in proportionately more women or members of the ethnic minority communities 'failing' the test and as a result their application is rejected and the use of the test cannot be justified, then this may be unfair discrimination. The onus of proof is on the employer to justify the use of the test.

To put it another way, if an employer sets a condition (for example, a test score of X or above) and a larger proportion of women or members of ethnic minority groups fail to meet this condition, compared to men or the ethnic majority group, the employer may be required to show that this condition is an essential requirement. If the use of the test can be shown to be justified, the result will be fair discrimination.

When an employer uses tests to select future employees, it is on the understanding that the test will differentiate between those candidates with the appropriate skills, knowledge and potential and those without them or at a lower level. Since a test that does not differentiate levels of abilities between candidates is of no real value to the employer, it is important to the employer that the right person is chosen for the right job. It is equally important to the candidate that it is the right job for him or her. Otherwise the candidate may not be happy in the job; even worse, he or she may not be capable of doing the job, which can be very demoralising. In such a case the person may have to look for another job and go through the whole selection process again.

So we can say that fair discrimination is about distinguishing between people, based on their abilities and aptitudes. These must be shown to be related to the job for which the tests are being used. What this means in practice is that, if an employer uses a particular test to identify a given set of abilities and aptitudes, these must be shown to be necessary to do the job. For example, it may need to be shown that high scorers do well in the job in question and that low scorers do not.

Reliability and validity

We said that tests can be useful if they are reliable and valid. So what do these two words mean in this context?

Reliability

We can say that a test is reliable when consistent results are obtainable. For example, tests that contain ambiguous questions are likely to be unreliable because different people would interpret the questions differently or the same person may even interpret them differently on different occasions.

Validity

Tests are said to be valid when they measure what the employer/user wants them to measure. In personnel selection terms it means that a test must be related in some way to the known demands of the job if it is to be of any use. For example, it needs to be shown that a test score predicts success or failure in a given job.

Figure 1.1 illustrates the kind of relationship that ought to exist between test scores and job performance, in which the higher the test score the better the performance in the job. In reality, however, it would be almost impossible to find such a high positive correlation. This is because of the difficulties in measuring job performance in many, if not most, types of job.

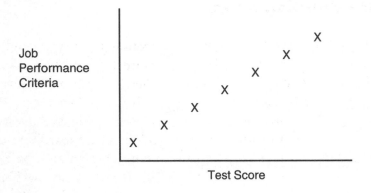

Figure 1.1 A positive correlation between test scores and job performance

Why do companies use tests?

There are a number of advantages to companies and other organisations from using psychometric tests. These include:

- Where an organisation receives a large number of applications, and because most selection tests are paper-and-pencil type, applicants can be tested in large groups. This is much more cost-effective than testing candidates individually.
- The recruitment and selection process can be a very costly affair, particularly if there is a high turnover of staff because of bad selection decisions, not to mention any other disruptions that may be caused. Thus it is in the interest of the company to choose the right people for the job. The use of tests can help in this process, provided, of course, that the tests are both valid and reliable.
- Tests can also lessen subjectiveness in assessing the applicant's potential to develop his or her aptitude for a

particular job. The lessening of subjectiveness in the selection process is also an advantage for applicants.

Test administration

Most tests are conducted under strict examination-type conditions. The main reason for this is to ensure that all candidates, at all times, are tested in the same manner. This is done so that no group is either advantaged or disadvantaged in terms of receiving the test instructions or in the way in which the tests are conducted. For example, one group might be allowed extra time to complete a test and so have an unfair advantage. There is thus a high probability that this group's average scores will be higher compared to those of a similar group of people who did not have this unfair advantage.

The process that is followed will be laid down by the test publishers. However, the majority of tests are likely to be conducted in the following way:

1. All candidates will be sitting facing the test administrator.
2. Candidates will be provided with all the materials necessary, such as pencils, erasers and answer sheets.
3. The tester will explain the purpose of the test or tests and also inform candidates how the test will be conducted.
4. The tester will read the instructions that need to be followed for the test. These instructions may also be written on the test booklet, in which case you should read them at the same time. In some tests the candidates are left to read the instructions by themselves. The reading time may be included in the test time or extra time may be given. Whichever method is used, it is strongly advised that you read and understand the instructions. Our experience has shown that many candidates fail to understand the test instructions and therefore make many errors in completing

the answer sheets. For example, some tests may require you to fill in two boxes on the answer sheet.

5. There will be a strict time limit. For the majority of tests, if not all, there is a time limit to which the tester will adhere. The tester may use a stopwatch; don't be put off by this. (Interest inventories and personality questionnaires do not usually have a strict time limit, though candidates are asked to complete them as quickly as possible.)

6. Many tests have example questions. In some tests the candidates are asked to attempt these, while in others the example questions have already been completed. In any case, their purpose is to ensure that the candidates understand what is required of them. Once again, make sure that you understand what you have to do.

7. In most tests candidates will be given the opportunity to ask questions. If you do not understand what is required of you, you should seek clarification. You should not feel intimidated about asking questions, no matter how trivial the question may seem. The chances are that there may be other people who have similar questions but who haven't plucked up enough courage to ask. So the motto is – ask; you have nothing to lose!

Test scores

So far we have discussed a number of issues concerning the background of tests. But now we need to address what happens once you have taken the test.

Naturally the test is scored; that is, it is marked. Once scored, the correct answers are added together. The result is called a 'raw score'. If there is more than one test then all the raw scores are noted. A set of tests is called a 'battery of tests'.

The raw score does not really mean anything on its own. This is because it does not tell us whether it is a good score or a bad score. For example, let us assume that candidate A gets 30 questions right out of a possible 50. So candidate A has a raw score of 30. If the test is easy and most people who are similar to him or her would have scored around 40, A's score is bad. On the other hand, if the test is a difficult one and most of the other people would have scored only around 20, candidate A's score is a good one.

Thus, for the scores to be meaningful we have to compare the individual's score with the scores of a similar group of people. This similarity could be in terms of age, level of education, background, etc. We would then be able to say that, compared to those people, this individual is either average, above average or below average.

We make this comparison by using what are called 'norm tables'. Norm tables tell us how other people have scored on a test. The group with whose scores we would compare an individual's score is called a 'norm group'. In a norm-referenced test the raw scores are compared with the scores of a norm group.

2

How to prepare for tests

Test publishers recognise that the candidate who has had lots of experience of selection tests has an advantage over a candidate who faces a test for the first time. The experienced or 'test-wise' candidate is likely to make fewer mistakes, understand the test demands better, be more confident, cope better with nerves, have developed a better test technique and be more likely to pass!

To counteract the advantage enjoyed by the test-wise, test descriptions are provided and they usually include practice questions. The idea is that the motivated candidate can practise on these questions and, therefore, have the same advantage as someone who has taken the test or a similar test before. The problem is that there are nearly always too few practice questions for the candidate to prepare thoroughly.

This is the main reason why we have produced this book. We feel that test publishers provide insufficient practice material to allow candidates to brush up properly their skills and abilities and so demonstrate their true potential.

Practice makes perfect

You will find in this book many practice questions. They are designed to help you brush up the types of skill examined in selection tests. They will also help you to become familiar with the kind of question and the exam-type conditions that apply in selection tests.

If you have to pass a sight test or if you need to pass a medical examination or be a certain height to get a job then there is no way that practice can help you to achieve these requirements. It is clearly absurd to suggest, for example, that you can improve your height through practice.

However, if you have to pass a test of your command of maths, English or basic science then practice can make a difference. If you are new to tests or if you need to brush up your maths, English or basic science then you are most likely to see the biggest improvements in your score.

We cannot say for certain that if you practise you will pass a selection test. But why not look at it this way: if you have been asked to sit a test then you have nothing to lose and possibly everything to gain if you undertake some test practice. It will help you to feel more settled and confident. It might mean that you build up your speed and accuracy and might help you to cope with any nerves. It will help you to demonstrate your true potential. It might mean you pass something you would otherwise have failed.

How best to practise

Education is the best sort of preparation for an employers' test. If you have just left full- or part-time study much of what you have done will have prepared you for these types of test.

Even if you have recently left education you can still benefit from practice. It will make you feel more settled about the test, and can also help you to brush up subjects that you may not have studied for some years. The most common of these is basic mental arithmetic. It is unusual for use of a calculator to be allowed in a selection test.

If it is some years since you undertook formal study or if you have done few or no employers' tests before then experience has shown us that up to 21 hours of practice can help.

The best type of practice is carried out on material that is very similar to the questions found in the real test. You should also try to get hold of material that allows you to practise on similar material under realistic test-type conditions.

If the test examines your command of basic science, or the vocabulary of science or maths, the material contained in this book will be of great benefit.

To be sure that you have the right kind of practice material you should read carefully the test description sent to you by the employer (if you have not received one then telephone and ask if they can provide you with details of the test).

Very often the test will be divided into sub-tests, each of which is separately timed and designed to measure a different ability. Make certain that you have practice material relevant to all the sub-tests.

If a selection of the test is not covered by the material in this book or if you want further material, please see 'Further reading' on page 180. Other useful sources are technical books with questions at the end of chapters, and the careers service may also have suitable material.

Organise your study

The benefit of practice is short-lived so you need to start close to when you have the test and continue right up to the day before. Concentrate on the skills that you are least good at. Try to be honest with yourself. If, for example, maths is your weakness then spend most time practising to build up your speed and accuracy in calculations. If the test description includes an example of a type of calculation that you cannot do then make sure you are able to do it when the day of the test arrives. You should aim to do in total between 12 and 21 hours of practice.

Your programme of work should look something like this:

- You are notified that you are going to have to sit the test.
- You read the test description carefully.
- You search for relevant test material.
- You undertake a series of practice sessions.
- You take the test.

Doing your best on the day

Go to bed early and try to get a good night's sleep. Do not drink alcohol. If you are unwell, telephone the organisation and try to arrange to sit the test on another day. You will not need pens or paper, as everything is supplied; however, it is important that you take with you your reading glasses or hearing aid if you wear them.

Leave home with plenty of time and go to the toilet before the test. Listen carefully to what the test administrator has to say. If you miss a point or do not understand something ask the administrator to repeat it.

It is highly likely that you will work through some practice questions before the real test starts. Don't worry if you get any of these examples wrong, as they do not count towards your score. Make sure, however, that you realise what you did wrong. If there is anything you do not understand ask the administrator to explain it. Don't be shy, as this is your last chance to have something explained to you. Once the test begins you will not be able to ask questions or get help.

Test strategies

During the real test it is very important that you do not waste time on questions to which you do not know the answer. If it is allowed, do all the easy questions first. Then, if you have time, go back to any questions you missed.

In multiple-choice papers, if you are not sure which is the correct answer it may help if you can rule out some of the suggested answers as wrong and then make an educated guess.

Make sure you indicate the answer in the way requested. Do not, for example, tick or cross the correct answer if the instructions ask you to circle it.

If you are placing your answers on a separate sheet, regularly check that you are placing your mark in the correct place. If, for example, you are doing question 9, make sure your answer is against the number 9 on the answer sheet.

Do not be surprised if you cannot answer all the questions in the given time. It is quite usual for there to be more questions than it is possible to answer.

Speed is of the essence so work as quickly as you can without rushing. This is where practice can really help.

In multiple-choice maths questions, estimating sometimes helps. Instead of trying to work out the exact answer to sums you find difficult, round the amount up or down to the nearest whole number.

You have to try hard to do well in a test

We cannot stress this enough. It is not only a matter of intelligence or aptitude. Your frame of mind is just as important. Push yourself; keep going and concentrating until you hear the words 'Stop now, please'. You really have to go for it in a selection test. The people who will pass are likely to be the candidates who are sitting poised ready to start; you can almost see the determination as they turn the page and get down to the questions. At the end of the test, if you do not feel drained by the exertion then you may not have done yourself justice.

What to do if you fail

Failing a test does not necessarily mean that you are incapable of doing the job or that you are not cut out for your chosen career. You may have failed by only one mark – that is how unfair these tests can seem. If you took the test again you might pass on your second attempt.

If you know what kind of career you want, do not let a negative test result discourage you into giving up your dream. We know this is easy to say but we have seen so many people pass having previously failed who have gone on to become perfectly good employees.

If you fail, get some advice. Go to your careers office or adviser; they are happy to help people of all ages. And try to find out about qualifications or courses that will help you to acquire the skills you need.

The chances are that an employer will not be willing to discuss your score with you or let you retake the test straight away. Find out when you can next apply and in the meantime work on the parts of the test in which you felt you did least well.

Apply to other organisations that recruit for similar positions – it may be that they do not use a test in their recruitment process. Even if they do, you may well do better in their test as you will be becoming 'test-wise'. Do lots of practice before you take another test.

3

Some of the most common types of technical tests

Categories of tests

Ability is the most common aspect of a candidate to be subject to testing, in the form of either paper-and-pencil tests or some practical exercise. These practical tests are sometimes referred to as performance tests or work sample tests. We talk about these on page 18.

Ability tests fall into two main categories: attainment tests and aptitude tests. Attainment is the candidate's current skills and knowledge. Aptitude is having either a talent for a particular skill or the potential to acquire it. It needs to be pointed out that the distinction between attainment tests and aptitude tests is not clear cut. Therefore, a single test can be used to measure either attainment or aptitude.

Attainment tests

Attainment tests are those that seek to assess how much skill and knowledge an individual has. For example, an arithmetic test for cashiers measures attainment as long as it is used to measure arithmetic and not used to measure performance as a cashier.

From an employer's point of view an attainment test may provide a better assessment than simply looking at past records of achievements or non-achievements as the case may be. A standardised test of arithmetic or spelling may give a more reliable indication of relevant present ability than a comparison of school qualifications in maths or English.

From a candidate's point of view an attainment test score will say more to an employer than simply talking about the candidate's skills. This is particularly useful when the candidate does not possess many, or even any, qualifications.

Aptitude tests

Aptitude tests are used to predict the potential of an individual for a particular job or a course of study. However, as mentioned above, it is not easy to separate tests of potential from tests of attainment because all forms of test assess the person's current skills and knowledge. But the results of that assessment may then be used in a variety of ways, for example:

- to highlight the individual's strengths and weaknesses;
- to provide career counselling;
- to predict success in a job or course.

Work sample tests

Work sample tests can be described as a miniature version of the job in question. The tasks encompass the main or major elements of a job. They are called work sample tests because that is the main purpose, and they are also practical. Hence they are sometimes referred to as performance tests.

Trainability tests

Another variation of the work sample test is the trainability test. Trainability testing is a method of assessing applicants' potential for learning new skills in a particular area.

Trainability testing is relatively common in technical positions, which often require the use of a range of hand tools and techniques. It is important that you take notes either when the task is being demonstrated or when instructions are given.

The types of tests that you are most likely to encounter are set out in the following sections.

Technical tests of verbal reasoning

These are about how well you understand ideas expressed in words and how you think and reason with words.

Examples of the types of question that may be asked

1. Fluid is to liquid as vapour is to _____.

A solid
B water
C gas
D dense
E not given

In this question you have to find out the association between the first two words and then apply the same principle to find the answer for the third word. The answer in this case is C, gas, because fluid and liquid have similar meanings, just as vapour and gas do.

2.   Fill in the missing word.
     If you can see through something it means that it is
     _____.

A opaque
B transparent
C vague
D familiar
E creative

3.   Two magnets with the same poles facing each other will
     _____ each other.

A repel
B attract
C expand
D contract
E not given

The answer to question 2 is B, transparent, and the answer to
question 3 is A, repel.

Technical tests of numerical reasoning

Like the verbal reasoning tests, the numerical reasoning tests
aim to identify strengths in understanding ideas expressed in
numbers and how well you think and reason with numbers.

Examples of technical numerical questions

1.   If five cathode ray tubes cost £400, how much does each
     one cost?

A £100
B £90
C £80
D £70
E £60

2.   If the sum of angles in a square is 360°, what is the size of each angle?

A 60°

B 70°

C 30°

D 90°

3.   In which two months were the same number of bearings sold?

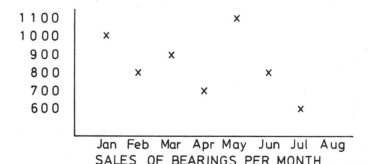

SALES OF BEARINGS PER MONTH

A Jan and Feb

B Feb and Apr

C June and Feb

D June and Apr

E Apr and May

The answers to the above questions are: 1. C; 2. D; 3. C.

Tests of diagrammatic reasoning

In tests dealing with diagrams, you will be presented with shapes and patterns from which you have to work out some kind of logical sequence in order to answer the question. The format of the questions is likely to involve your being presented with five shapes or patterns with one of the figures missing. Underneath or beside these figures you will find a further five shapes or patterns from which you will have to select one as the missing answer. Look at the examples below.

Examples of diagrammatic reasoning questions

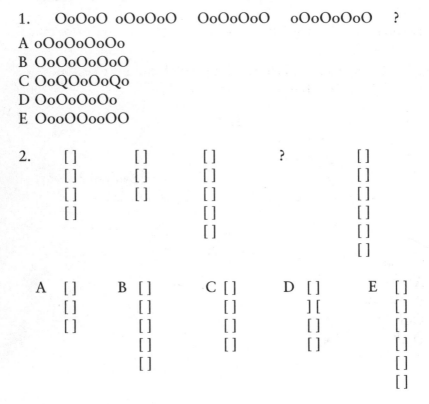

1.   OoOoO oOoOoO   OoOoOoO   oOoOoOoO   ?

A oOoOoOoOo
B OoOoOoOoO
C OoQOoOoQo
D OoOoOoOo
E OooOOooOO

2.   [ ]   [ ]   [ ]   ?   [ ]
      [ ]   [ ]   [ ]   [ ]
      [ ]   [ ]   [ ]   [ ]
      [ ]   [ ]   [ ]
                           [ ]   [ ]
                                               [ ]

   A [ ]   B [ ]   C [ ]   D [ ]   E [ ]
      [ ]   [ ]   [ ]   ] [[ ]
      [ ]   [ ]   [ ]   [ ]   [ ]
                [ ]   [ ]   [ ]   [ ]
                [ ]   [ ]
                                             [ ]

The answers are: 1. B; 2. C.

Tests of mechanical reasoning

Dealing with mechanical concepts (principles of transmitting movement).

Examples of mechanical reasoning questions

1.   Which of the following will weigh the most:
      1 kg feathers, 1 kg steel bar, 1 kg stone?

A the feathers
B the steel bar
C the stone
D equal

2.   In the diagram below, which switch(es) must be closed to
      light up the bulb?

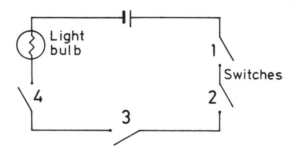

A 1
B 2
C 3
D all
E any one

3.   In which direction will B turn?

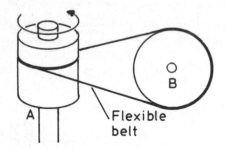

A clockwise
B anticlockwise
C will not turn

The answers are: 1. D; 2. D; 3. B.

The above list is not of course exhaustive. However, these are the main types of question that you are likely to come across under the heading of technical tests.

4

Other types of test that you may encounter

You will find that, regardless of the type of test you are taking, verbal and numerical tests will be part of the test battery. You will also find that the words and numbers used will relate to the type of job or course you are applying for. Thus for technical tests the majority of the words in the verbal section will be of a technical nature, whereas in an IT-related test the words will be those used in computing, and so on.

Examples of other tests are:

- *Tests of clerical skills*. These deal with checking and classifying data, speedily and accurately.
- *Tests of IT skills*. These investigate the candidate's ability to follow set rules and instructions, sequence events into logical order and interpret flow charts.
- *Personality questionnaires*. These aim to identify certain stable characteristics.
- *Interest inventories or interest blanks*. These aim to identify an individual's interest in particular occupations.

Personality questionnaires (or tests)

Many people refer to personality inventories or questionnaires as tests. This, however, is misleading, since to talk about personality questionnaires as tests implies that there is a pass or fail score, which obviously is not the case.

It would appear that personality is something that everyone talks about. One often hears people talk about someone having a 'great personality', but what exactly is it?

There is no one theory or definition of personality with which all psychologists agree, but most personality question-naires aim to identify certain stable characteristics. They are based on the assumption that the responses will be represen-tative of how an individual will react in a given social situation, particularly the one in which the selector is interested, ie the organisation or department in which that individual may be working.

The main characteristics that personality questionnaires aim to identify in an individual are:

Extroversion	*Introversion*
Tough minded	Tender minded
Independent	Dependent
High self-confidence	Low self-confidence

Interest inventories (or tests)

Strictly speaking 'interest tests', like 'personality tests', are not tests at all, because they are not about obtaining a good or a bad score, nor about passing or failing. It is for this reason that they are usually referred to as interest inventories or interest ques-tionnaires. The aim of these interest inventories is to find out an individual's interest in particular occupations.

Interest inventories will cover interests in activities such as:

- *Scientific/technical* – how and why things work or happen. Types of job: different kinds of engineers and technicians.
- *Social/welfare* – helping or caring for people. Types of job: youth/community worker, nurse, teacher/instructor, social worker.
- *Persuasion* – influencing people and ideas or selling goods and services. Types of job: salesperson, manager, advertising.
- *Arts* – designing or creating things or ideas. Types of job: writer, clothes designer, painter.
- *Clerical/computing* – handling data, systems. Types of job: administrator, bookkeeper.

The use of interest inventories is limited compared to, say, aptitude tests in the selection of applicants. This is because the inventories appear, at least on the face of it, easy to fake. For example, if a person is applying for a position as a clerk, he or she may deliberately indicate a stronger interest in tasks related to the office environment.

The interest inventories are probably most useful in vocational guidance where, one assumes, people are less likely, if at all, to fake them.

5

The technical selection tests essential dictionary

To do well in a technical test you must be familiar with the basic vocabulary of science and engineering. The best kind of practice comes from reading textbooks and discussing the subject in a classroom or at work. It will also help if you commit meanings to memory.

Below you will find approximately 150 words. It is essential that you know their meanings. All are taken from the basic vocabulary of technical subjects and often come up in tests.

The definitions offered are intended only as a reminder of the meaning. If you are new to any of them you may need to refer to specialist textbooks. Quick study guides and revision books for GCSE physics are especially useful.

Before you take a technical test make sure you know the meanings of the following words:

abrasion   The effect on a surface of grinding by a hard or scraping substance.

abrasive   Material that can be used to cut, smooth or polish. Sandpaper is an abrasive material.

accelerator   The pedal or lever that increases the speed of a vehicle.

acrylic   A type of plastic that is usually transparent. It can be hard and used in place of glass.

adhesion   The sticking together of two or more surfaces.

adhesive   A substance used to make materials stick to each other. Glue is an adhesive.

aerial   An object used for the transmission or receiving of radio waves.

alloy   A mixture of two or more pure metals.

alternating current   An electric current that flows alternately in one direction and then the other.

aluminium   A lightweight metal from the bauxite ore.

ammeter   The instrument used to measure electric current.

ampere   A unit of measurement. It is used to measure electrical current.

anode   An electrode with a positive charge.

arc   A curve, in particular any part of the circumference of a circle.

architect   A person who designs and plans buildings and other structures.

area   The space occupied by a surface.

assembly   Where two or more parts fit together. Also the act of fitting parts together.

atmospheric pressure   The weight of all the air in the atmosphere. It changes according to how high you are and with the weather. Normally atmospheric pressure is taken to be the pressure of the air at sea level.

axis   A line or rod through the middle of a spinning object.

axle   A spindle on which, or with which, a wheel or wheels revolve.

balance   An instrument used to weigh objects.

barometer   Instrument for measuring atmospheric pressure, used in the forecasting of weather and ascertaining height above sea level.

battery   Electric cells connected together to provide current.

beam   A horizontal strong point, for example a joist used in the construction of floors and ceilings.

bearing   A machine part used to reduce friction at the point where a rotating shaft and its support bear on each other. Types of bearing include, for example, plain, ball and roller.

bevel gears   Cone-shaped gears used to connect shafts that meet at an angle, normally a right angle (90°).

bimetallic   Two metals one on top of the other, bound together to form a strip.

biodegradable   Material or substance that will rot or decompose over a period of time.

block and tackle   An arrangement of ropes or chains and pulleys used to provide mechanical advantage in the lifting of heavy loads.

bracing   A network of wire or rope used to hold a structure firmly.

bracket   A projecting support for a shelf or other structure that requires support from beneath.

brake   A device to slow down or stop a moving part or object.

brass   A yellowish metal, an alloy of copper and zinc, that is non-magnetic.

cam   A component that is used to convert rotary motion into linear. It has an off-centre axis or an irregular shape.

cantilever   A beam that is only supported at one end. A diving board is an example of this.

capacitor   A device used to accumulate electric charge.

cast   Liquid materials are poured into moulds so that they solidify to form shapes, which may be quite complex.

catalyst   A substance that aids a chemical change in other substances but does not undergo change itself.

cathode   A negatively charged electrode.

ceramic   An article of, for example, clay or porcelain hardened by being baked; non-metallic materials that are hard, brittle and poor conductors.

chisel   A sharp tool used to cut or shape wood or stone.

circle   A closed plane curve; a line that is always equidistant from a point; a round enclosure.

circuit   An insulated path – often of copper – through which an electric current passes.

circumference   The distance around the outside of a circle.

clamp   A device used to hold things firmly while being cut, drilled or glued together.

coarse   Something that is rough.

cohesion   Sticking together; force with which molecules stick together; tendency to remain united.

combustion   Destruction by fire; development of light and heat going with chemical oxidation of organic tissue.

component   Something that is a part of a structure or mechanism.

composite   A thing that is made of two or more other materials, which in some way makes it better than the individual materials.

compound   Mixture of elements; substance consisting of two or more elements chemically united.

compression   A force that squashes something.

concave   A term applied to lenses or mirrors that have a surface curved inwards.

condensing   Reducing from gas or vapour to liquid.

cone   A three-dimensional figure with a flat circular base tapering to a point.

convex   A term applied to lenses or mirrors that have a surface curved outwards.

copper   A reddish-brown pure metal. It is a good conductor of electricity and therefore is used extensively in all things electrical. Also used widely as water pipes.

corrugated   Materials that are shaped so that they have ridges and grooves. This gives materials extra strength.

coupling   A joint that allows objects to be linked together; a joint that ensures motion is transferred from one part to another.

crank   A right-angled bend in a shaft that is used to change the direction of motion.

cross-section   The view of the surface formed when a three-dimensional object is cut across.

cube   A three-dimensional square; a box; a solid contained by squares.

cylinder   A three-dimensional shape with straight sides and a circular base, top and cross-section.

density   Compactness of substance; how heavy it is; a measure by ratio between mass and volume.

diameter   Measured by drawing a straight line from one side to the other of any body or geometric figure, for example a circle – the line must pass through its centre.

die   A tool used to cut, shape or mould resistant material into a desired shape.

diode   An electrical component that allows current to pass through in one direction only.

direct current   Electric current flowing in one direction only.

disassemble   Take something apart in a systematic way so that it can be assembled back in its original form without any bits left over.

dismantle   Take something to pieces.

dissolve   Make or become liquid, especially by immersion in a liquid. Often this involves the dissolving of a solid into a liquid.

distort   Bend or twist something out of shape.

drill   A rotating cutting bit used in drills. Also means to make a round hole in wood, metal or other hard material.

dye   Change the colour of a material by soaking it in a coloured solution.

dynamo   A machine that converts mechanical energy into electric energy by rotating coils of copper in a magnetic field.

eccentric   Not precisely circular, for example a cam deliberately off-centre used to push open valves is eccentrically mounted; idiosyncratic.

efficiency   The amount of useful work performed, expressed in relation to the amount of energy expended.

elastic   An elastic material can be squashed, squeezed or stretched but return to its original shape.

electrical   Anything that uses or is involved with electricity is electrical.

electrolysis   The process by which electric current passes through a liquid that conducts electricity.

electron   One of the fundamental constituents of matter; a subatomic particle with a negative charge.

element   A substance that cannot be divided into simpler substances by chemical means.

energy   The capability of doing work.

engineer   A person who designs, builds or maintains machines, engines or structures.

equilibrium   The state of balance; something that is balanced.

etch   Engrave a pattern on the surface of a glass or metal using acid or other chemical.

expansion   Increase in volume caused by heat.

ferrous   A metal that contains iron. It is usually magnetic but not always.

file   A metal hand tool with small sharp teeth on its surface that is for smoothing wood, plastic and metal.

flame retardant   Material that has been treated with special chemicals so that it does not catch fire very easily. However, if it does catch then it will burn much more slowly.

flammability test   A test to see how quickly a material catches fire and how fast it burns.

flux   A substance used in soldering to keep the metal clean and stop it from oxidising.

force   A push or a pull that changes the state or position of a body.

forge   Change the shape of a metal by heating and hammering.

friction   The resistance that a body meets when moved across another body or surface.

fulcrum   Point on which a lever is placed to get purchase or on which it turns or is supported.

fuse   In most cases a thin piece of metal with a low melting point, which melts if subjected to an ampage above a known amount.

gear   A toothed wheel used to transmit motion or change the direction or speed of motion.

graph   A diagram illustrating two or more variables and the relation that exists between them.

gravity   A force of attraction between items of separated matter; the falling of objects dropped; the property of having weight.

gyrate   Move in a circular manner; rotate.

hacksaw   A saw that is used to cut metals and plastics. Its blade can be replaced if worn or broken.

hardboard   Wood fibres compressed to form a thin sheet.

helix   A spiral curve, for example the thread of a screw; a curve that winds around the outside of a cylinder.

hexagon   A shape with six sides and six angles.

horizontal   A line or object that is parallel to the horizon; level or flat.

hydraulic   Liquids in motion; machinery operated by force transmitted through a liquid.

idler   A gear wheel that connects two other gears in order to make them both rotate in the same direction.

injection moulding   A process where liquid material is forced, under pressure, into a mould and allowed to harden. Plastic and metal parts are made in this way.

insulate   Prevent or reduce the passage of electricity or heat.

isometric projection   An engineer's drawing; a method for producing a three-dimensional representation of an object.

kilo   Means one thousand, as in kilogram, kilometre.

latent   Hidden, concealed, existing but not manifest, for example latent heat.

lathe   A machine that can be used to shape wood, metal or plastic by rotating it against a sharp tool.

lever   A bar or rod used to provide mechanical advantage. One point (the fulcrum) is fixed, another is connected to the force (weight) to be resisted or acted on and a third point is connected with the force (power) applied.

lubricant   A fluid applied in order to reduce friction.

machine   An apparatus for applying mechanical power; it will comprise several parts, each with a definite function.

magnet   Iron or iron ore, which attracts iron (iron-based materials) and points magnetic north and south when suspended.

malleable   Where a material can easily be shaped or moulded.

mallet   A type of hammer made from soft material.

mass-production   The process of manufacturing large quantities of products.

material   Matter from which things are made, raw, unmanufactured.

meter   An instrument that is used to measure current, voltage or resistance.

molecule   The smallest portion to which a compound substance can be reduced without losing its chemical identity.

molten   Metal, plastic or glass that has been heated until it becomes very soft or liquid.

obscure   Indistinct, not clear, hidden, remote from observation.

ohm   A measure of electrical resistance.

optical fibre   A glass fibre that is very fine and flexible, through which light signals can travel.

ore   A mineral or rock from which a metal can be extracted.

oscillate   Move to and fro between two points.

parallel   Lines that are continuously the same distance apart, for example railway lines.

pendulum   A weight mounted to swing freely under the influence of gravity.

pentagon   A five-sided figure with five angles.

perpendicular   Very steep, erect, upright.

pivot   Short shaft or pin on which something turns or oscillates.

plastic   A general term for synthetic materials made from oil.

plywood   Several thin sheets of wood glued together to form a stronger sheet of timber.

pulley   A set of wheels set in a block used to change the direction of force or provide mechanical advantage.

pyramid   A three-dimensional figure with a square base and sloping sides that meet at a point or apex.

radius   Straight line from the centre to the circumference of a circle or sphere.

ratchet   A mechanism that allows a toothed wheel to rotate in one direction only.

reflect   Throw back off the surface of a body, in particular heat, light and sound.

reinforce   Use extra materials to make something stronger.

resistant   Materials that are difficult to cut, bend, drill or manipulate.

safety rule   A type of ruler that protects the fingers when cutting materials with a craft knife.

shaft   A rotating rod that transmits motion or power.

shear   A strain produced by pressure in a structure or substance.

solid   Of stable shape; of three dimensions; not a liquid or gas; not hollow.

spelter   A high-melting-point solder made from copper and zinc.

spindle   Another word for axle and kingpin; a rod that rotates and is used to support, for example, wheels.

spring   A coil or hair, usually metal, that if compressed returns to its original shape.

sprocket   A toothed wheel that is used to engage a chain on, for example, a bike.

spur gear   This has straight teeth and is the most common type of gear.

square   A four-sided figure with sides of equal length.

structure   Something that resists loads or forces. Buildings, bridges and the human skeleton are examples of structures.

strut   A rigid tube or bar that makes a structure more stable.

switch   A device that opens or closes an electric circuit.

synthetic   Human-made; made up of artificial compounds rather than those extracted from, for example, plants.

tension   Stress caused by pulling on a bar or cord etc.

thermometer   Instrument for measuring temperature.

thermostat   A device that controls temperature automatically.

timber   A general term for wood.

tolerance　An allowance for variation in the dimensions of a machine.

torque　A turning force; any force that causes rotation.

torsion　A twisting or turning force.

toxic　A substance that is poisonous or harmful in some way.

triangle　A three-sided figure with three angles.

vacuum　Pressure below that of the atmosphere. In some cases the pressure within an enclosed space can be considerably below atmospheric pressure.

vaporising　The changing of a liquid into a gas.

velocity　Quickness; rate of motion; speed in a given direction.

vibrate　Move to and fro, oscillate; move rapidly and unceasingly.

vice　A tool for holding materials while being cut, filed, drilled or planed.

volt　A unit for measuring electric force.

volume　Solid content; bulk.

watt　A unit of power.

wavelength　The distance between the peaks or troughs of any two waves. Sound and light are transmitted in waves.

work　A result of force moving an object in the same direction as the force. Machines do work.

X and Y axes　The horizontal (X) and vertical (Y) axes on a two-dimensional graph.

Technical numerical questions

Section one

Try the questions below under timed conditions. Allow yourself 10 minutes and see how many questions you can do. It is likely that you will not be able to complete all the 30 questions in this time. Do not worry, as most tests are designed so that the majority of people do not complete all the questions in the time allowed.

You should not spend too long on any one question; instead move on and if there is time you can come back to any questions that you have not done. In this way you will avoid wasting time and therefore have a chance of attempting all the questions, some of which you will find easier than others. This way your score may be better than if you waste time on questions that you find difficult.

Before you start make sure that you will not be disturbed and have a watch in front of you so that you can time yourself properly. Do not go over the 10-minute time limit.

Now turn over the page and begin the test.

Q1. If a set of five screwdrivers costs £4, how much does each
     screwdriver cost?

A 50p
B 60p
C 70p
D 80p
E 90p

Answer

Q2. If 1 kilogram is equivalent to approximately 2.2 imperial
     pounds, how many pounds are there in 5 kilograms?

A 10
B 10.2
C 11.2
D 11
E 10.8

Answer

Q3. How many 100 g steel bars would you have in 1 kg?

A 10
B 11
C 12
D 13
E 14

Answer

Q4. If 12 inches equals 1 foot, how many inches are there in 5 feet?

A 40 inches
B 50 inches
C 60 inches
D 70 inches
E 55 inches

Answer

Q5. If 10 mm is equal to 1 cm, how many millimetres are there in 50 centimetres?

A 50 mm
B 500 mm
C 5,000 mm
D 550 mm
E 50,000 mm

Answer

Q6. If a train travels at 90 miles per hour, how many miles will it travel in 20 minutes?

A 20 miles
B 30 miles
C 40 miles
D 50 miles
E 35 miles

Answer

Q7. If a manufacturing company employs 500 people of
      whom 20% are women, how many women work there?

A 20
B 50
C 100
D 150
E 200

Answer

Q8. What is the ratio of women to men in the above
      company?

A 1:2
B 1:3
C 1:4
D 1:5
E 1:6

Answer

Q9. Assuming that a printer can print 5 characters per second,
      how many characters would it be able to print in 2
      minutes?

A 300
B 500
C 600
D 700
E 900

Answer

Q10. Assume that you can print 400 words on a sheet of A4-size paper. How many A4-size sheets of paper would you need to print 6,000 words?

A 10
B 13
C 15
D 18
E 20

Answer [   ]

Q11. If a 90-litre tank needs to be filled up using a hosepipe that allows water to flow at 2 litres per second, how many seconds would be needed to fill the tank?

A 180 seconds
B 90 seconds
C 45 seconds
D 22.5 seconds
E 11.25 seconds

Answer [   ]

Q12. If a lathe rotates at 600 rpm, how many times does it rotate in 1 second?

A 60
B 40
C 20
D 10
E 5

Answer [   ]

Q13. If the above lathe is able to rotate at twice the speed, how many times would it be able to rotate in 1 second?

A 60
B 40
C 20
D 10
E 5

Answer

Q14. If a car tyre costs £19.95 how much would it cost for a set of four plus a spare tyre?

A £99.99
B £99.00
C £99.75
D £95.00
E £99.95

Answer

Q15. If a discount of 10% is given on the total cost on the above tyres, how much money would be saved?

A £9.99
B £9.90
C £9.75
D £9.50
E £9.09

Answer

Q16. Three computers each need to have a different circuit board replaced. The costs are £125, £150 and £175. What is the average cost per board?

A £450

B £250

C £150

D £125

E £175

Answer _____

Q17. A technical magazine subscription costs £36 per annum. What is the cost of a single magazine?

A £5

B £4

C £3

D £2

E £1

Answer _____

Q18. What is the total area of the two rectangles?

A 450 cm^2

B 850 cm^2

C 950 cm^2

D 900 cm^2

E 1,800 cm^2

Answer _____

Q19. If a quarter of a box is shaded, what percentage of the whole does this represent?

A 20%
B 25%
C 30%
D 35%
E 40%

Answer

Q20. An electric saw turns at a speed of 120 revolutions per minute. How many revolutions will it have made at the end of 15 minutes?

A 1,200
B 1,400
C 1,600
D 1,800
E 2,000

Answer

Q21. If a train covers 380 miles in 4 hours, what would its average speed have been?

A 80 mph
B 85 mph
C 90 mph
D 95 mph
E 75 mph

Answer

Q22. An electric water pump is able to pump water at a rate of 12 gallons per minute. How long would it take to fill a 900-gallon tank?

A 1 hr
B 1 hr 30 min
C 1 hr 15 min
D 2 hr
E 45 min

Answer

Q23. What is the combined area of the rectangles below?

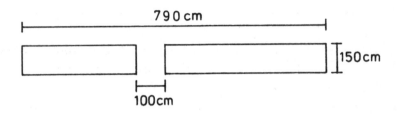

A 1.50 m²
B 13.35 m²
C 7.90 m²
D 11.85 m²
E 10.35 m²

Answer

Q24. See the graph below. If the income from the sale of cars was £28,000, how many cars must have been sold?

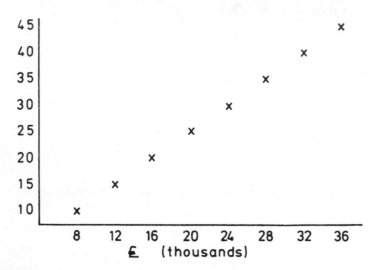

£   (thousands)

A 25
B 30
C 35
D 40
E 45

Answer

Q25. See the graph above. If a salesperson gets 10% on all his or her sales, how much commission can be earned if 20 cars are sold?

A £120
B £160
C £1,200
D £1,600
E £16,000

Answer

Q26. Assume a lorry is able to hold a load of 350 kg. If a load of only 175 kg is put on the lorry, what percentage of its total capacity is being wasted?

A 35%

B 40%

C 45%

D 50%

E 55%

Answer

Q27. An electric fan rotates at 70 rpm at speed setting 1 and rotates at 120 rpm at speed setting 2. What is the difference in speed in rpm between the two?

A 70 rpm

B 65 rpm

C 60 rpm

D 55 rpm

E 50 rpm

Answer

Q28. At speed setting 3 the above fan rotates at 180 rpm. How much faster is speed setting 3 in relation to speed setting 2, expressed as a percentage?

A 50%

B 33%

C 60%

D 40%

E 66%

Answer

Q29. A computer operator is able to input 120 characters per minute using a standard keyboard. How many characters can be typed in half an hour?

A 360
B 3,600
C 36,000
D 1,200
E 12,000

Answer

Q30. If a computer floppy disk is able to hold 720,000 characters, how many characters would 10 disks hold?

A 720,000
B 72,000
C 7,200,000
D 14,000,000
E 14,200,000

Answer

Section two

It is unlikely that you will be allowed to use a calculator in a test so if you rely on one put it aside and undertake lots of practice without it to build up your speed and accuracy in mental arithmetic. Only use a calculator to check your answers. So many people fail maths tests not because they are unable to do the questions but because they cannot do them quickly enough or because they make too many avoidable mistakes. Practice can make all the difference between pass and fail for these candidates.

You may need to learn or relearn your multiplication tables before you reach the required speed and accuracy.

Practice maths

Work out the number or symbol and write your answer in the answer box. (Remember, do not use a calculator.)

Q1. $9 - 3.6 + 4 = ?$

Answer

Q2. $? = 7 \times 38$

Answer

Q3. $? \times 6 = 20 + 16$

Answer

Q4.   158 – 6 = 129 + ?

Answer

Q5.   102 – 96 = 18 ÷ ?

Answer

Fact: To convert inches to centimetres you multiply by 2.54.

Q6.   How many centimetres are there in 50 inches?

Answer

Q7.   2.4 × 6.6 = ?

Answer

Q8.   3 ? 2.1 = 9.3 – 3

(*Clue:* Your answer should be either plus, minus, divide or multiply.)

Answer

Q9.   30% of 70 = ?

Answer

Q10. ? = 27 × 36

Answer

Q11. 7 + 2 = 17 ? 8

Answer [ ]

Fact: To convert grams to pounds you multiply by 0.0022.

Q12. How many pounds are equivalent to 5,000 grams?

Answer [ ]

Q13. How many grams are there in 2.2 pounds?
(*Clue:* in this case you divide by 0.0022.)

Answer [ ]

Q14. 68 × 0.7 = ?

Answer [ ]

Q15. 7 × 16 = 28 × ?

Answer [ ]

Q16. 40% of 30 = ?

Answer [ ]

Q17. 5.5 × 6 = 330 ÷ ?

Answer [ ]

Q18. $300 - ? = 7 \times 16$

Answer [   ]

Q19. $26 - ? = 9.3$

Answer [   ]

Q20. $35 ? 17 = 95 + 500$

Answer [   ]

Tip: To convert imperial tons to kilograms you multiply by 1,016.

Q21. How many kilograms are there in an imperial ton?

Answer [   ]

Q22. How many kilograms are there in 7 imperial tons?

Answer [   ]

Fact: To convert gallons to litres you multiply by approximately 4.5.

Q23.   Approximately how many litres of water are required to fill a 5-gallon bucket?

Answer [   ]

Q24. Approximately how many gallons are equivalent to 18 litres?

Answer

Some tests require you to demonstrate that you can deal with quantities. Try the following examples (express all answers in centimetres).

Fact: 10 millimetres (mm) = 1 centimetre (cm); 100 cm = 1 metre (m).

Q25. 10 cm + 3 m + 16 mm = ?

Answer

Q26. 5 cm – 7 mm + 1 m = ?

Answer

Q27. 22 mm + 6 cm + ? = 2 m

Answer

Q28. 215 mm – 5 mm + 1.5 m = ?

Answer

Q29. ? + 100 cm +16 mm = 2.5 m

Answer

Q30. 5 × 3m lengths of wood – ? = 2,400 mm

Answer

Practice test

Over the page you will find a multiple-choice mock test comprising 20 questions.

Allow yourself six minutes in which to attempt the 20 questions.

To each question a choice of answers is suggested, one of which is correct. It is your task to select one of the suggested answers and write it into the answer box.

Do not turn the page until you are ready.

Q1.   86 – 14 = 9 + ?

A 62
B 63
C 64
D 65

Answer

Q2.   23 – 17 = ? ÷ 6

A 35
B 36
C 37
D 38

Answer

Q3.   5 ? 1 = 20 ÷ 5

A Minus
B Plus
C Multiply
D Divide

Answer

Q4.   16 + 75 ÷ 7 = ?

A 10
B 11
C 12
D 13
E 14

Answer

Q5.   ? + 68 = 16 × 9

A 75

B 76

C 77

D 78

E 79

Answer

Q6.   9 × ? = 63

A 4

B 5

C 6

D 7

Answer

Q7.   ? × 12 = 48

A 1

B 2

C 3

D 4

Answer

Q8.   45% of 70 = ?

A 30

B 30.5

C 31

D 31.5

Answer

Q9.   47 × 19 = ?

A 873
B 883
C 893
D 903

Answer

Q10. 9 × 6 + 33 = 3 ? 8 +76

A Minus
B Plus
C Multiply
D Divide

Answer

Q11. 8 × 9 = ? + 15

A 54
B 55
C 56
D 57

Answer

Q12. 212 − 43 = ? + 9

A 160
B 161
C 162
D 163

Answer

Q13. 7 × 2.5-metre lengths of wood – 500 cm = ? + 300 mm

A 12.2 m

B 14.8 m

C 16.7 m

D 17 m

Answer

Q14. 73 – ? = 40 ÷ 5

A 64

B 65

C 66

D 67

Answer

Q15. How many pounds are equivalent to 2,000 grams? (To convert grams to pounds multiply by 0.0022.)

A 4.1

B 4.2

C 4.3

D 4.4

Answer

Q16. If a 120-litre tank is filled using a hosepipe that allows water to flow at a rate of 3 litres a minute, how long will it take to fill the tank?

A 20 minutes
B 40 minutes
C 60 minutes
D 80 minutes

Answer

Q17. How many centimetres are there in 15 inches? (To convert from inches to centimetres multiply by 2.54.)

A 37.8
B 37.9
C 38
D 38.1

Answer

Q18. How many kilograms are there in 5 imperial tons? (To convert from imperial tons to kilograms multiply by 1,016.)

A 5,040
B 5,060
C 5,080
D 5,100

Answer

Q19. One million has how many zeros?

A 4

B 5

C 6

D 7

Answer

Q20. Approximately how many litres of fuel are required to fill a 19-gallon tank? (To convert approximately between gallons and litres multiply by 4.5.)

A 85.5 litres

B 86 litres

C 86.5 litres

D 87 litres

Answer

Area, volume and surface areas

Success in many technical tests requires you to be able to calculate area, volume and surface area for complex shapes made up from the basic squares, cubes, rectangles, cuboids and triangles. Try the following 27 examples to revise the basics. Then try the further questions that are typical of the sort used to select apprentices in the construction industry.

Q1.   What is the area of a square with 4-cm-long sides?

4 cm

A 4 cm^2
B 8 cm^2
C 12 cm^2
D 16 cm^2

Answer

Q2.   What is the area of a square with 2.5-cm-long sides?

2.5 cm

A 2.5 cm^2
B 5 cm^2
C 6.25 cm^2
D 10 cm^2

Answer

Q3. What is the area of a square with 12-cm-long sides?

12 cm

A 24 cm^2
B 48 cm^2
C 60 cm^2
D 144 cm^2

Answer

Q4. What is the length of the perimeter of a square with sides of 12 cm?

12 cm

A 12 cm
B 24 cm
C 36 cm
D 48 cm

Answer

Q5. What is the length of the perimeter of a rectangle 2 cm
high and 3 cm long?

2 cm

3 cm

A 8 cm
B 10 cm
C 12 cm
D 14 cm

Answer

Q6. Use the information provided to calculate the length of
the perimeter of this shape:

Information: The square has sides 2 cm long; the rectangle is 8
cm long and 4 cm high.

A 28 cm
B 29 cm
C 30 cm
D 31 cm

Answer

Q7.   What is the volume of a cube with sides 2 cm long?

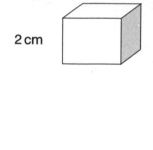

2 cm

A 4 cm^3
B 6 cm^3
C 8 cm^3
D 10 cm^3

Answer

Q8.   What is the volume of a cube with sides 4 cm long?

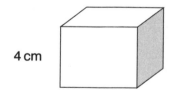

4 cm

A 16 cm^3
B 24 cm^3
C 64 cm^3
D 96 cm^3

Answer

Q9. What is the volume of a cube with sides 6 cm long?

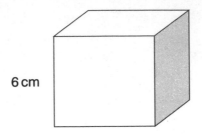

6 cm

A 12 cm^3
B 36 cm^3
C 72 cm^3
D 216 cm^3

Answer

Q10. How many sides does a cube have?

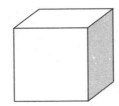

A 3
B 4
C 5
D 6

Answer

Q11. What is the surface area of a cube with 2-cm-long sides?

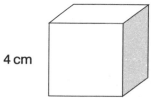

2 cm

A 16 cm^2
B 20 cm^2
C 24 cm^2
D 28 cm^2

Answer

Q12. What is the surface area of a cube with sides 4 cm long?

4 cm

A 16 cm^2
B 20 cm^2
C 24 cm^2
D 28 cm^2
E 96 cm^2

Answer

Q13. What is the surface area of a cube with sides 6 cm long?

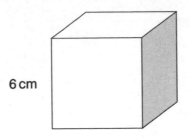

6 cm

A 180 cm^2
B 216 cm^2
C 252 cm^2
D 288 cm^2

Answer

Q14. What is the volume of the cuboid below?

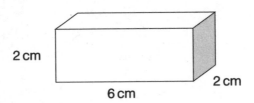

2 cm

6 cm

2 cm

A 12 cm^3
B 24 cm^3
C 36 cm^3
D 48 cm^3

Answer

Q15. What is the volume of this cuboid?

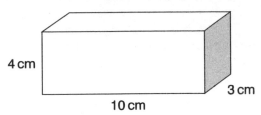

A 120 cm^3
B 80 cm^3
C 34 cm^3
D 19 cm^3

Answer

Q16. Calculate the volume of this cuboid.

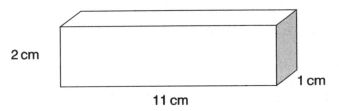

A 121 cm^3
B 88 cm^3
C 44 cm^3
D 22 cm^3

Answer

Q17. How many sides of this cuboid are identical?

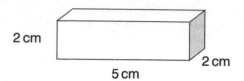

2 cm

5 cm

2 cm

A All six
B Three identical pairs of sides
C A pair of identical sides and four other identical sides

Answer

Q18. How many sides of this cuboid are identical?

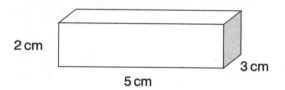

2 cm

5 cm

3 cm

A All six
B Three identical pairs of sides
C A pair of identical sides and four other identical sides

Answer

Q19. What is the surface area of the following cuboid?

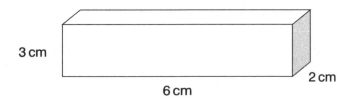

2 cm

5 cm

2 cm

A 61 cm^2
B 59 cm^2
C 48 cm^2
D 35 cm^2

Answer

Q20. What is the surface area of the following cuboid?

3 cm

6 cm

2 cm

A 90 cm^2
B 72 cm^2
C 66 cm^2
D 51 cm^2

Answer

Q21. What is the surface area of the following cuboid?

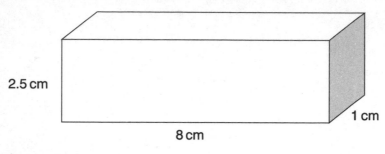

A 61 cm²
B 62 cm²
C 63 cm²
D 64 cm²

Answer

Q22. Calculate the area of the following right-angled triangle:

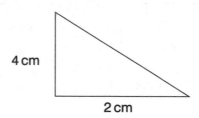

A 2 cm²
B 4 cm²
C 6 cm²
D 8 cm²

Answer

Q23. Calculate the area of the following right-angled triangle:

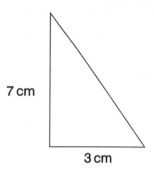

A 9 cm^2
B 9.5 cm^2
C 10 cm^2
D 10.5 cm^2

Answer

Q24. Calculate the area of the following right-angled triangle:

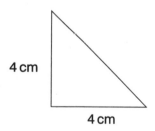

A 4 cm^2
B 8 cm^2
C 12 cm^2
D 16 cm^2

Answer

Q25. What is the area of this equilateral triangle?

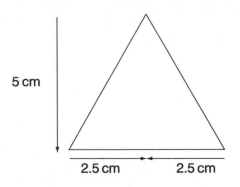

2.5 cm   2.5 cm

Answer

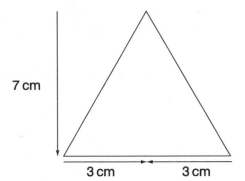

3 cm   3 cm

Q26. What is the area of this isosceles triangle (two sides are of equal length)?

Answer

Q27. What is the area of this isosceles triangle?

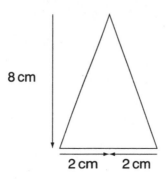

Answer

Trainability and selection tests in construction

The following questions are typical of psychometric tests used to select apprentices in the construction industry. They require you to be confident and accurate in the calculation of areas, surface areas and volumes, which we have just reviewed.

You are required to study the shape and answer the questions that follow it.

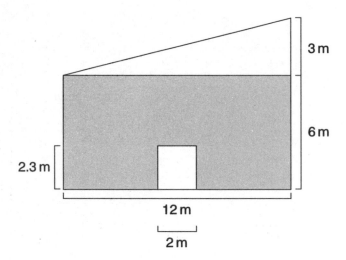

Q1. What is the area of the shaded part of this shape (excluding the area of the door)?

Answer

Q2. What is the area of the roof part of this shape?

Answer

Q3. What is the area of the door part of this shape?

Answer

Q4. How much paint would you require to paint the shaded area of this shape if 1 litre of paint covered 20 m²?

Answer

Q5. What is the area of the doorway and three identical windows in this shape?

Answer

Q6. What is the area of the roof part of this shape?

Answer

Q7. What is the area of the shaded part of this shape (excluding the doors and windows)?

Answer

Q8. Excluding the doorway and windows what is the total area of this shape?

Answer

Q9. How many 1-litre tins of paint would you need to paint the shaded area of the shape if a litre of the paint covered 20 m² ?

Answer

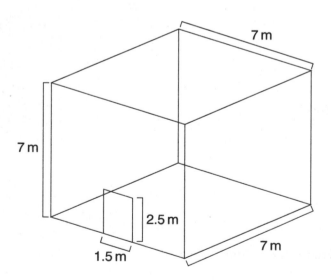

Q10. What is the volume of this room?

Answer [ ]

Q11. What is the surface area of the walls of the room (exclude the area of the door from your answer)?

Answer [ ]

Q12. What is the area of the floor of this room?

Answer [ ]

Q13. How much paint would you require to paint two coats on the walls of this room if the coverage of 1 litre of the paint was 20 m² (give your answer to one decimal place)?

Answer [ ]

Q14. What is the volume of this room?

Answer [ ]

Q15. What is the area of the ceiling of this room?

Answer

Q16. What is the surface area of the walls of this room (excluding the space taken up by the door and window)?

Answer

Q17. How much paint would you require to paint the ceiling of this room if 1 litre of paint covered 25 m²?

Answer

Electrical power

In the following exercise you are required to work out the power when you are given the voltages and currents.

The formula for working this out is: P = V × I (power = voltage × current). For example, if you have 10V (voltage) and 5A (current), P = 10 × 5. Therefore power equals 50 W (watts).

Note: Power is measured in watts and current in amperes.

Now try the following.

Exercise 1

Q1. P = 7V × 4A   Answer

Q2. P = 9V × 6A   Answer

Q3. P = 15V × 7A   Answer

Q4. P = 25V × 9A   Answer

Q5. P = 55V × 10A   Answer

Q6. P = 130V × 25A   Answer

Q7. P = 240V × 12A   Answer

Q8. P = 110V × 13A   Answer

Q9. P = 150V × 30A   Answer

Q10. P = 160V × 5A   Answer

Exercise 2

In this exercise you are given the power values and currents. You have to work out the voltages.

For example, 10W = V × 2A. Here you have to change the formula around. V = W ÷ A (you are now dividing power by current). So the answer is 5V.

Find the voltage for the following power and current (answers to 2 decimal places).

Q1. P = 50W and I = 10A   Answer

Q2. P = 75W and I = 15A   Answer

Q3. P = 150W and I = 25A   Answer

Q4. P = 230W and I = 20A   Answer

Q5. P = 110W and I = 11A   Answer

Q6. P = 650W and I = 65A   Answer

Q7. P = 240W and I = 12A   Answer

Q8. P = 130W and I = 5A   Answer [   ]

Q9. P = 195W and I = 13A   Answer [   ]

Q10. P = 150W and I = 15A   Answer [   ]

Exercise 3

In this exercise you are going to work out the current. You will be given the power and voltages.

The formula this time will be I = P ÷ V.

Answers correct to 2 decimal places.

Q1. P = 400W and V = 68V   Answer [   ]

Q2. P = 385W and V = 56V   Answer [   ]

Q3. P = 1,200W and V = 12V   Answer [   ]

Q4. P = 855W and V = 49V   Answer [   ]

Q5. P = 760W and V = 16V   Answer [   ]

Q6. P = 495W and V = 18V   Answer [   ]

Q7. P = 285W and V = 8V   Answer

Q8. P = 474W and V = 40V   Answer

Q9. P = 670W and V = 65V   Answer

Q10. P = 890W and V = 48V Answer

Exercise 4

In this exercise we are going to look at resistance, voltage and current. The formula is R = V ÷ I.

R = resistance (measured in ohms – represented by the symbol Ω).

Work out the resistance for the following values of voltages and current.

Q1. Voltage = 10V and current = 2A   Answer

Q2. Voltage = 6V and current = 3A   Answer

Q3. Voltage = 8V and current = 2A   Answer

Q4. Voltage = 3V and current = 3A   Answer

Q5. Voltage = 12V and current = 2A   Answer

Q6. Voltage = 12V and current = 4A   Answer [   ]

Q7. Voltage = 9V and current = 3A   Answer [   ]

Q8. Voltage = 1V and current = 4A   Answer [   ]

Q9. Voltage = 5V and current = 10A   Answer [   ]

Q10. Voltage = 10V and current = 5A Answer [   ]

Exercise 5

In this exercise we are going to work out the voltage. The figures for resistance and current will be given.

The formula will change slightly: V = R × I (voltage = resistance × current).

Q1. Resistance = 15Ω and current = 15A
                                    Answer [   ]

Q2. Resistance = 10Ω and current = 5A
                                    Answer [   ]

Q3. Resistance = 16Ω and current = 12A
                                    Answer [   ]

Q4. Resistance = 19Ω and current = 14A

Answer ☐

Q5. Resistance = 20Ω and current = 15A

Answer ☐

Q6. Resistance = 25Ω and current = 17A

Answer ☐

Q7. Resistance = 35Ω and current = 13A

Answer ☐

Q8. Resistance = 45Ω and current = 15A

Answer ☐

Q9. Resistance = 9Ω and current = 1A

Answer ☐

Q10. Resistance = 5Ω and current = 5A

Answer ☐

Exercise 6

Here we are going to work out the current. The figures for resistance and voltages are given.

I = R × V (current = resistance × voltage).

Q1. Resistance = 15Ω and voltage = 30V

Answer ▢

Q2. Resistance = 15Ω and voltage = 3V

Answer ▢

Q3. Resistance = 6Ω and voltage = 4V

Answer ▢

Q4. Resistance = 5Ω and voltage = 30V

Answer ▢

Q5. Resistance = 16Ω and voltage = 3V

Answer ▢

Q6. Resistance = 14Ω and voltage = 6V

Answer ▢

Q7. Resistance = 6Ω and voltage = 9V

Answer ▢

Q8. Resistance = 4Ω and voltage = 8V

Answer ▢

Q9. Resistance = 18Ω and voltage = 18V

Answer ▢

Q10. Resistance = 8Ω and voltage = 3V

Answer [   ]

Exercise 7

The formula you will need is E = P × T (energy = power × time).
   Example: E = P (2kW) × T (2 hours). Answer = 4kWh.

   In this exercise you are going to work out how much energy (measured in kilowatt-hours) is used for each of these periods of time for a 2kW appliance.

Q1. 2 hours   Answer [   ]

Q2. 3 hours   Answer [   ]

Q3. 3.5 hours   Answer [   ]

Q4. 6 hours   Answer [   ]

Q5. 12 hours   Answer [   ]

Q6. 2.5 hours   Answer [   ]

Q7. 1.5 hours   Answer [   ]

Q8. 7 hours   Answer [   ]

Q9. 8.5 hours   Answer   [   ]

Q10. 9.5 hours   Answer   [   ]

Q11. half a day   Answer   [   ]

Q12. one day   Answer   [   ]

Q13. quarter of a day Answer   [   ]

Q14. one-third of a day Answer [   ]

Q15. 180 minutes   Answer   [   ]

Q16. 30 minutes   Answer   [   ]

Q17. two days   Answer   [   ]

Q18. 12.5 hours   Answer   [   ]

Q19. 4 hours   Answer   [   ]

Q20. 7.5 hours   Answer   [   ]

Exercise 8

The formula you need is $P = E \div T$.

In this exercise you have to work out the power output of appliances that transfer these amounts of energy in 4 hours.

Q1. 7 kWh   Answer

Q2. 12 kWh   Answer

Q3. 32 kWh   Answer

Q4. 2 kWh   Answer

Q5. 6 kWh   Answer

Q6. 3 kWh   Answer

Q7. 46 kWh   Answer

Q8. 90 kWh   Answer

Q9. 48 kWh   Answer

Q10. 8kWh   Answer

Q11. 68kWh   Answer

Q12. 56kWh   Answer

Q13. 34kWh   Answer

Q14. 78kWh   Answer

Q15. 97kWh   Answer

Q16. 29kWh   Answer

Q17. 49kWh   Answer

Q18. 76kWh   Answer

Q19. 27kWh   Answer

Q20. 15 kWh   Answer

Technical verbal questions

This chapter comprises practice examples of the types of question that test your command of the basic vocabulary of science and engineering.

For some of the questions we have suggested time limits so that you can practise against the clock.

If you have learnt the essential dictionary (Chapter 5) you should be able to answer many of these questions.

Basic vocabulary of science and engineering

The first 10 questions test your knowledge of synonyms (words that mean the same).

Q1. Which of the following words means the same as eccentric?

A normal
B dull
C idiosyncratic
D energetic
E none of these

Answer ▭

Q2. Which of the following words means the same as corrode?

A correspond
B protect
C rust
D insulate
E corrupt

Answer ▭

Q3. Which of the following words means the same as sequence?

A series
B sequel
C random
D secretive
E disorder

Answer ▭

Q4. Which of the following words means the same as variable?

A striped
B constant
C stable
D changeable
E steady

Answer

Q5. Which of the following words means the same as flexible?

A stiff
B pliable
C current
D immovable
E hollow

Answer

Q6. Which of the following words means the same as compress?

A condense
B spread
C impress
D expand
E pressure

Answer

Q7. Which of the following words means the same as saturate?

A dry
B gratify
C soak
D rainfall
E heat

Answer

Q8. Which of the following words means the same as invert?

A shy
B transpose
C equilibrium
D straighten
E transport

Answer

Q9. Which of the following words means the same as fluctuate?

A smooth
B vary
C liquid
D immobile
E level

Answer

Q10. Which of the following words means the same as precise?

A unclear
B guess
C accurate
D wrong
E none of these

Answer

The following types of question test your knowledge of the vocabulary of science by posing straightforward multiple-choice questions.

Q11. When light enters glass and changes direction this bending of light rays is called?

A reflection
B absorption
C transmission
D refraction
E deviation

Answer

Q12. Stored energy waiting to do work is called?

A potential energy
B inert energy
C kinetic energy
D nuclear energy

Answer

Q13. Speed in a stated direction is called?

A distance
B vectors
C newtons
D gradient
E acceleration

Answer

Q14. The flow of heat through a material without the material
     itself moving is called?

A insulation
B refraction
C reflection
D bimetallic
E conduction

Answer

Q15. When atoms of different elements link they form?

A neutrons
B protons
C molecules
D magnets
E solids

Answer

Q16. The measure of the amount of matter in an object is called the:

A kilogram
B atoms
C volume
D mass
E area

Answer [   ]

Q17. A push or pull that one object applies to another is called a:

A force
B mass
C velocity
D physics
E density

Answer [   ]

With the next type of question you have to choose a word from the suggested answers that best completes the sentence. You are sometimes offered the answer 'none of these'; select this if you believe none of the other answers is correct.

Choose the word that best completes the following sentences:

Q18. Electrons have a _____ charge.

A positive
B magnet
C negative
D neutron
E massive

Answer

Q19. An electrical fuse is a short, thin piece of _____.

A current
B wire
C pipe
D power
E liquid
F none of these

Answer

Q20. A _____ object is said to be in equilibrium.

A heavy
B clockwise
C balanced
D gravity
E pivot

Answer

Q21. _____ is needed to change liquid to vapour.

A Insulation
B Velocity
C Cold
D Heat
E Gas

Answer [   ]

Q22. Steam _____ to form water.

A evaporates
B melts
C condenses
D boils
E fuses

Answer [   ]

Q23. Each moving or vibrating molecule has _____ energy.

A kinetic
B random
C molecular
D microscope

Answer [   ]

Q24. Friction is the _____ a body meets when moving across another body or surface.

A energy
B efficiency
C resistance
D mass
E law

Answer

Q25. A body gyrates when it moves in a _____ manner.

A constant
B circular
C straight
D vertical
E lively

Answer

Q26. _____ prevents or reduces the passage of electricity or heat.

A Insulation
B A pivot
C Hydraulics
D A magnet
E A dynamo

Answer

Q27. The rate of _____ of a body is called its velocity.

A vibration
B reflection
C work
D resistance
E motion

Answer

Q28. A substance that aids a chemical change in other bodies but does not undergo change itself is called a _____.

A gas
B bimetallic
C catalyst
D synthetic
E category

Answer

Q29. An alloy is a mixture of two or more pure _____.

A metals
B liquids
C substances
D solids
E gases

Answer

Q30. _____ pressure changes depending on how high you are and with the weather.

A surface
B barometer
C electrical
D work
E gravitational
F atmospheric

Answer

Q31. When an object is _____ its molecules vibrate violently.

A frozen
B obscure
C heated
D circular
E stretched

Answer

Q32. _____ zero is the lowest possible temperature that can be reached.

A Kelvin
B Centigrade
C Absolute
D Freezing
E Cold

Answer

Q33. _____ is a body's power of doing work by virtue of its
   motion.

A Safety
B Vitality
C Friction
D Density
E Energy

Answer

Q34. In an element all atoms are _____.

A identical
B molecules
C stretched
D gases
E idiosyncratic

Answer

Q35. Evaporation occurs at the _____ of a liquid.

A surface
B throughout
C molecules
D boiling-point
E none of these

Answer

Until they get used to them, most people have difficulty with the next type of question.

You have to work out the relationship that exists between the first pair of words and then apply that relationship to the third word and the suggested answers.

We have provided you with an example below. In this instance the relationship between change and stability is that they are opposites, so you have to look for the opposite of 'special', which is 'mundane'.

The relationship is not always one of opposites; it could be, for example, that they mean the same or one is a quality of the other.

We have given you over 30 practice questions so that you can undertake lots of practice.

Example

Q36. Change is to stability as special is to:

A multiple
B particular
C mundane
D progress
E peculiar

Answer C

Q37. Car is to petrol as cooker is to:

A battery
B heat
C food
D gas
E kitchen

Answer

Q38. Square metres are to area as cubic metres are to:

A velocity
B length
C distance
D height
E volume

Answer

Q39. Clockwise is to anticlockwise as forward is to:

A vector
B opposite
C reverse
D upwards
E equilibrium

Answer

Q40. North Pole is to South Pole as anode is to:

A cathode
B positive
C diode
D negative
E magnet

Answer

Q41. Frequency is to hertz as energy is to:

A metre
B work
C joule
D degree
E watt

Answer

Q42. Screwdriver is to screw as hammer is to:

A spanner
B nail
C cog
D plug
E mallet

Answer

Q43. Ohm is to resistance as watt is to:

A volt
B pressure
C force
D amplification
E power

Answer

Q44. Ball is to sphere as box is to:

A triangle
B square
C circle
D cube
E solid

Answer

Q45. Sphere is to circle as cube is to:

A box
B rectangle
C square
D house
E none of these

Answer

Q46. Hurricane is to wind as monsoon is to:

A tropics
B storm
C rain
D sunshine
E none of these

Answer

Q47. Wallet is to bank as shopping bag is to:

A supermarket
B cashpoint
C vegetables
D building society
E none of these

Answer

Q48. Body is to blood as engine is to:

A car
B muscles
C combustion
D oil
E none of these

Answer

Q49. Straight is to crooked as intact is to:

A symmetrical
B broken
C horizontal
D complete
E none of these

Answer

Q50. See-through is to transparent as intact is to:

A glass
B opaque
C drink
D complete
E none of these

Answer

Q51. Water is to irrigate as light is to:

A illuminate
B electricity
C bulb
D river
E none of these

Answer

Q52. Centimetre is to ruler as ounce is to:

A inch
B scales
C pound
D rubber
E none of these

Answer

Q53. Fat means the opposite of:

A wide
B thin
C big
D short
E none of these

Answer

Q54. Straight means the opposite of:

A long
B flat
C horizontal
D bent
E none of these

Answer

Q55. Frozen means the opposite of:

A solid
B melted
C water
D ice
E none of these

Answer

Q56. Constant means the opposite of:

A intermittent
B continuous
C often
D always
E none of these

Answer

Q57. Nervous means the opposite of:

A confident
B scared
C cautious
D silent
E none of these

Answer

Q58. Effervescent means the opposite of:

A bubbly
B turbulent
C pocket
D tasty
E still

Answer

Q59. Gram is to kilogram as metre is to:

A length
B kilometre
C mile
D ruler
E speed

Answer

Q60. Kilometres per hour are to speedometer as degrees centi-
    grade are to:

A weather
B heat
C thermometer
D Fahrenheit
E miles

Answer

Q61. Second is to minute as day is to:

A hour
B week
C night
D clock
E millisecond

Answer

Q62. Circle is to sphere as square is to:

A pyramid
B plane
C triangle
D rectangle
E cube

Answer

Q63. Kilojoules are to energy as hectares are to:

A area
B electricity
C agriculture
D volume
E current

Answer

Q64. Second is to time as litres are to:

A space
B solids
C volume
D fluid ounces
E atoms

Answer

Q65. Millibars are to pressure as degrees centigrade are to:

A temperature
B weather
C barometer
D velocity
E wind

Answer

Q66. Metre is to distance as watt is to:

A volt
B power
C second
D time
E momentum

Answer

Q67. Condense is to cool as evaporate is to:

A heat
B liquid
C freeze
D solid
E cool

Answer

Q68. One is to two as radius is to:

A diameter
B circumference
C three
D angle
E circle

Answer

Basic principles of physics

Below are 32 technical verbal questions that review your knowledge of the basic principles of physics. Use these questions to revise some of the facts and principles of physics that are widely known amongst candidates of technical tests.

Q1.   Which force(s) act between molecules?

A attractive forces
B repulsive force
C both

Answer

Q2.   Energy is measured in:

A seconds
B joules
C centigrade
D metres

Answer

Q3.   Metals are good _____ of heat.

A conductors
B insulators
C convectors

Answer

Q4. Impurities _____ the melting point of water.

A lower

B increase

C do not change

Answer

Q5. A dull black surface is a _____ of radiation.

A good absorber

B poor absorber

Answer

Q6. An increase in pressure _____ the boiling point of water.

A lowers

B increases

Answer

Q7. The moon is _____ .

A illuminated

B a luminous object

Answer

Q8. Sound is caused by _____.

A resonance
B vibration
C echoes
D diffraction

Answer

Q9. If you look into a plane mirror and touch your right eye,
     which eye does your image appear to touch?

A your right eye
B your left eye

Answer

Q10. The statement 'Extension is directly proportionate to a
     stretching force' is an expression of which law?

A Boyle's law
B Charlie's law
C Hooke's law
D Newton's third law
E Murphy's law

Answer

Q11. A TV remote control transmits _____.

A radio waves
B ultraviolet
C visible light
D infrared

Answer [   ]

Q12. Which of the following forms of radiation are affected by
an electric field?

A alpha
B beta
C gamma

Answer [   ]

Q13. Which component from the list can be used to make a
photographer's light meter?

A light-emitting diode
B light-dependent resistor
C thermostat
D reed switch

Answer [   ]

Q14. Put the following planets in the correct order, working away from the Sun.

A Saturn
B Venus
C Earth
D Mercury
E Uranus

Answer [   ]

Q15. A gun is fired and the echo heard after 3 seconds. How far away is the object from which the sound reflected? (Speed of sound in air is 340 m/s.)

A   1,020 m
B   2,040 m
C   510 m

Answer [   ]

Q16. At what temperature will water boil at the top of Mount Everest? (Look to the suggested answers and use your understanding of physics to help work it out.)

A   100 °C
B   120 °C
C   35 °C
D   70 °C

Answer [   ]

Q17. Starting with the colour with the longest wavelength, put the colours from the visible spectrum in the correct descending order.

A indigo
B red
C blue
D orange
E violet
F yellow
G green

Answer

Q18. How long does it take light to travel from the Sun to the Earth?

A 2 seconds
B 8 minutes
C 24 hours

Answer

Q19. Put the following into the correct order to describe the energy transfer that occurs when you connect an electric motor to a battery.

A electric energy
B kinetic energy
C potential energy from the load
D chemical energy

Answer

Q20. Which of the following radioactive materials is used in domestic smoke detectors?

A strontium 90
B americium 241
C cobalt 60

Answer

Q21. What is the human body temperature in kelvin?

A 273K
B 310K
C 37K

Answer

Q22. What is the radius of the Earth?

A 12,800 km
B 3,200 km
C 6,400 km

Answer

Q23. What magnetic material is used to make computer disks and videotapes?

A steel
B iron oxide
C pure iron
D silicon

Answer

Q24. How long does light take to travel from our sun to the nearest star?

A 4 years
B 12 months
C 36 hours
D 8 years

Answer

Q25. Electrostatic paint spraying exploits which character-istic(s) of electricity?

A unlike electric charges attract
B like electric charges repel
C both
D neither

Answer

Q26. An object has a volume of 36 cubic metres and a density of 920 kg/m³. What is its mass?

A 153.3 kg
B 33,120 kg
C 926 kg

Answer

Q27. When light enters glass it changes direction. This bending of light rays is called _____.

A deviation
B absorption
C refraction

Answer

Q28. What is the latent heat of vaporisation of water?

A the amount of energy required to boil away 1 kilo of water to steam
B the amount of energy needed to melt 1 kilo of ice to water
C neither of these

Answer

Q29. If a weight weighed 1 kg on Earth, how much would the scales register if the same weight was weighed on the Moon?

A 1.5 kg
B 0 kg
C 166.6 g

Answer

Q30. An astronaut feels weightless when orbiting the Earth because:

A the astronaut is beyond the gravitational pull of the Earth
B the astronaut and the spacecraft are falling at the same rate

Answer ☐

Q31. For a fixed mass of gas at a constant temperature, which of the following are true?

The volume depends on the pressure.

The volume is inversely proportional to the pressure.

If the pressure is doubled the volume is halved.

Boyle's law describes the relationship.

A all are true
B three out of four are true
C two are true
D only one statement is truc

Answer ☐

Q32. A firework transfers _____ energy to thermal energy.
A elastic
B kinetic
C electrical
D chemical

Answer ☐

8

Tests of diagrammatic reasoning

Diagrammatic reasoning tests require you to find a missing shape or pattern from a set of figures that form a logical sequence. Diagrammatic tests are also referred to as abstract reasoning tests because they do not have any verbal or numerical content, apart from the instructions. In other words, all the questions are picture (shapes and patterns) based, with no words or numbers.

Here you will find diagrammatic reasoning example questions followed by a timed exercise.

The format of the questions

You will be presented with shapes and patterns from which you have to work out a logical sequence of events in order to answer the question. The format of the question is likely to be that you are presented with five shapes or patterns with one of these figures missing. Underneath or beside these figures you will find a further five shapes or patterns from which you will have to select one as the missing answer. Here are two examples for you to consider:

Example questions

1. [ ]   [ ]   [ ]   ?   [ ]
    [ ]   [ ]   [ ]   [ ]
               [ ]   [ ]   [ ]
                          [ ]   [ ]
                                              [ ]
                                              [ ]

    A   B   C   D   E
    [ ]   [ ]   [ ]   [ ]   [ ]
    [ ]   [ ]   [ ]   [ ]   [ ]
    [ ]   [ ]   [ ]   [ ]   [ ]
    [ ]   [ ]   [ ]   ] [[ ]
    [ ]   [ ]   [ ]   [ ]
               [ ]   ] [

2. [ ] [ ]   [ ] [ ]   [*] [ ]   [ ] [*]   ?
    [ ] [*]   [*] [ ]   [ ] [ ]   [ ] [ ]
    A   B   C   D   E
    [ ] [ ]   [ ] [*]   [ ] [ ]   [*] [ ]   [ ] [ ]
    [*] [ ]   [*] [ ]   [ ] [*]   [ ] [*]   ] [[*]

Answers to the example questions are: 1. A; 2. C.

Practice test

On the next page you will find 19 diagrammatic reasoning questions. You should attempt to do these in five minutes, so before you start make sure that you will not be disturbed and also make sure that you have a clock or a watch so that you can time yourself.

Ensure that you understand what is required of you; if not, look at the above examples again. Once you have started, work as fast as you can and don't spend too long on any one question.

When you are ready, start the test.

Q1.

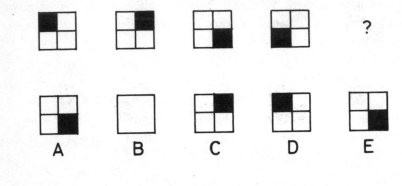

Answer [   ]

Q2.

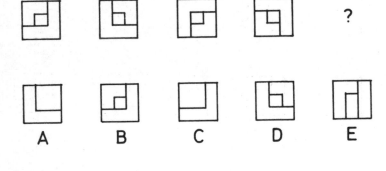

Answer [   ]

Q3.

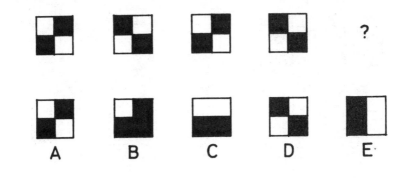

Answer [   ]

Q4.

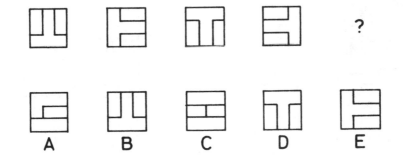

Answer [   ]

Q5.

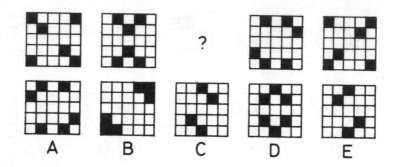

Answer [   ]

Q6.

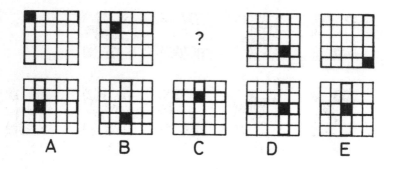

Answer [   ]

Q7.

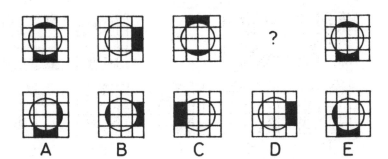

Answer

Q8.

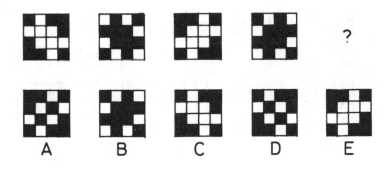

Answer

Q9.

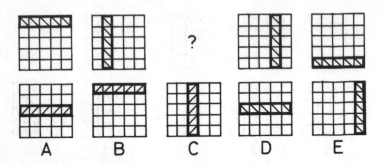

Answer [   ]

Q10.

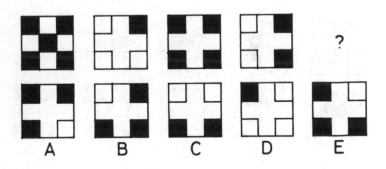

Answer [   ]

Q11.

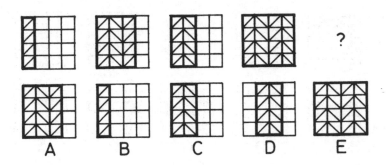

Answer [   ]

Q12.

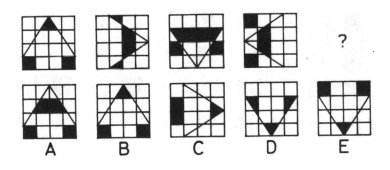

Answer [   ]

Q13.

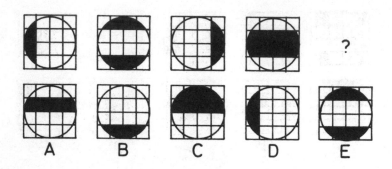

Answer [   ]

Q14.

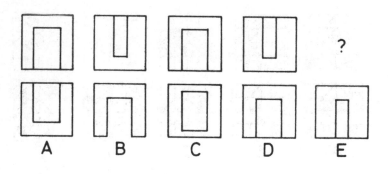

Answer [   ]

Q15.

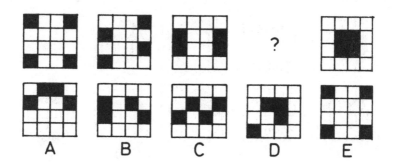

Answer [   ]

Q16.

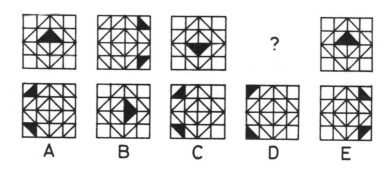

Answer [   ]

Q17.

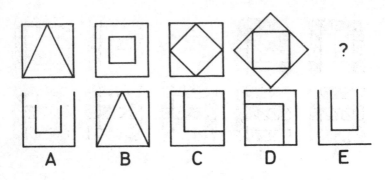

Answer [   ]

Q18.

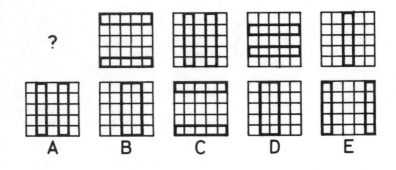

Answer [   ]

Q19.

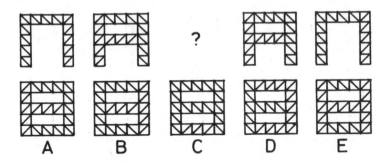

Answer [   ]

9

Mechanical questions

Section one

The questions in this section are based on the principles of mechanics, that is how things work and function.

Example questions

1. If B turns in an anticlockwise direction which way will A turn?

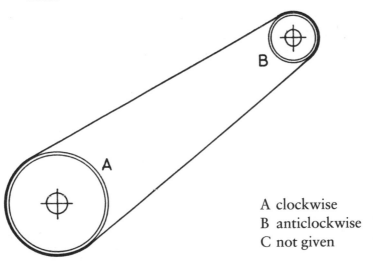

A clockwise
B anticlockwise
C not given

2.   If a person facing north turns 90 degrees clockwise, what direction will that person be facing?

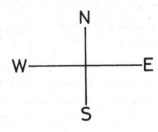

A north
B east
C west
D south

Answers to the example questions are: 1. B; 2. B.

Practice test

Over the page you will find 15 mechanical reasoning test questions. These should be done to a strict time limit. You should try to do as many as you can in five minutes.

Remember to make sure that you won't be disturbed in the middle of the test and also be certain to time yourself accurately.

You should work as quickly and as thoroughly as you can, but don't spend too long on any one question.

When you are ready, turn over the page and begin.

Q1. Which switch(es) would you need to close to light up the
     bulb?

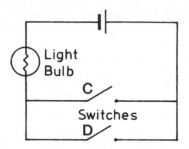

A C
B D
C either

Answer

Q2. If the left-hand-side wheel rotates in the direction shown,
     which way will the other wheel turn?

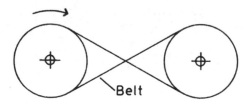

A same direction
B opposite direction
C won't turn

Answer

Q3.   Which point will balance the plank?

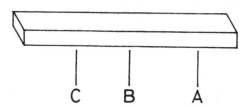

A   A
B   B
C   C

Answer

Q4.   If a person facing south turns 180 degrees in a clockwise
      direction, which way will that person be facing?

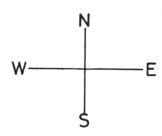

A north
B east
C west
D south

Answer

Q5. If you were facing south and turned 360 degrees, what direction would you be facing?

A north
B east
C west
D south

Answer

Q6. Which circuit has a serial connection?

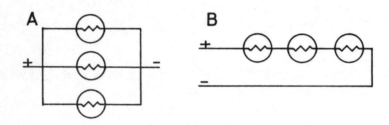

Answer

Q7. What will happen to the two horse-shoe magnets? Will they:

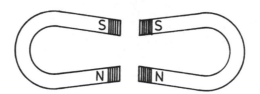

A attract each other
B repel each other
C not given

Answer

Q8. If you wanted A to turn in a clockwise direction, which way would B have to rotate?

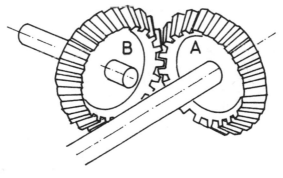

A anticlockwise
B clockwise
C same direction as gear A

Answer

Q9. Which chain is bearing the most stress of the weight?

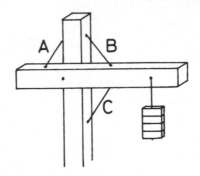

A A
B B
C C
D all equally

Answer

Q10.   Which of the following statements is true?

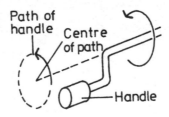

A smaller crank; smaller movement; easy to turn
B bigger crank; bigger movement; easy to turn
C size is not important

Answer

Q11. If a magnet is placed as shown, in which direction will the compass needle point?

A east
B west
C north
D south

Answer

Q12. Which pair of magnets will attract each another?

A	S| MAGNET |N		N| MAGNET |S	
B	N| MAGNET |S		S| MAGNET |N	
C	S| MAGNET |N		S| MAGNET |N	

A A
B B
C C

Answer

Q13. If gear B rotates in a particular direction, which direction, in relation to each other, will A and D rotate?

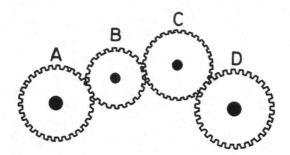

A in the same direction as each other
B in the opposite direction to each other
C always clockwise
D always anticlockwise

Answer

Q14. By looking through this, objects will appear:

Magnifying glass

A smaller
B bigger
C same size

Answer

Q15. A rotates in the opposite direction to C; B rotates anti-clockwise. In which way will D turn?

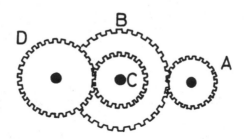

A clockwise
B anticlockwise
C same as C

Answer

Section two

Below are some more practice mechanical questions for which we have not suggested any time limits. Go over carefully any you get wrong. If there are some you do not understand it often helps to discuss them.

Try to make sure you understand the principle on which the question is based. You may need to undertake further reading. We would recommend any of the quick-study or teach-yourself-physics books. For details ask at your local bookshop or library.

Q16. Which planet will have the longest orbit of the star?

A planet A
B planet B
C planet C
D you cannot tell

Answer　　　[   ]

Q17. If all the planets orbit in the same amount of time which
will be travelling the most slowly?

A planet A
B planet B
C planet C
D you cannot tell

Answer

Q18. Which planet is likely to have the hottest climate?

A planet A
B planet B
C planet C
D you cannot tell

Answer

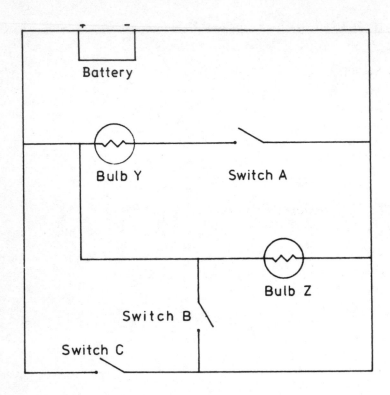

Q19. Which switch would you need to close in order to light bulb Y?

A Switch A
B Switch B
C Switch C

Answer [   ]

Q20. Which switch would you need to close to light both bulbs
Y and Z?

A Switch A
B Switch B
C Switch C

Answer

Q21. Is it possible to light only bulb Z?

A yes
B no
C cannot tell

Answer

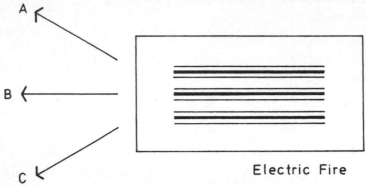

Electric Fire

Q22. In which direction would the convected heat travel?

A A
B B
C C
D all directions

Answer _____

Q23. In which direction would the radiated heat travel?

A A
B B
C C
D all directions

Answer _____

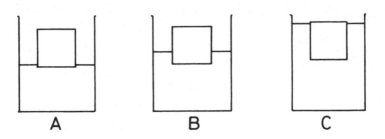

Q24. If in each instance the object consists of the same substance then which liquid has the greatest specific gravity?

A A
B B
C C
D they are all the same

Answer

Q25. If all three beakers contain identical liquids which object would be heaviest?

A A
B B
C C
D they are all the same

Answer

Q26. With which lever will it be easier to lift the cupboard?

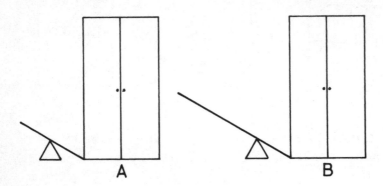

A A
B B
C neither

Answer

Q27. If the fly wheels are rotated at the same speed which
would be the hardest to stop?

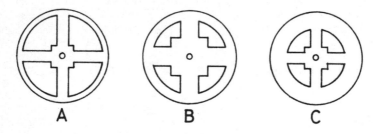

A A
B B
C C

Answer

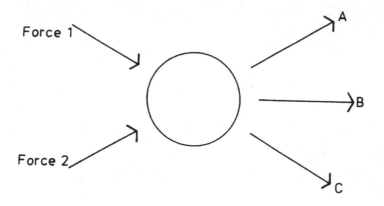

Q28. If Force 1 and Force 2 are equal in which direction would
the ball move?

A A
B B
C C

Answer

Q29. If Force 1 is greater in which direction is the ball most
likely to move?

A A
B B
C C

Answer

Q30. Which best illustrates the way in which light will be affected by the lens?

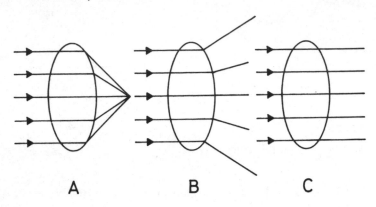

A   A
B   B
C   C
D   none of these

Answer

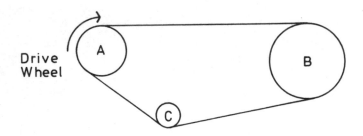

Q31. Which way will wheel B turn?

A anticlockwise
B clockwise

Answer

Q32. Which wheel will make the most revolutions in 60
seconds?

A A
B B
C C

Answer

Q33. Which weight is the heaviest?

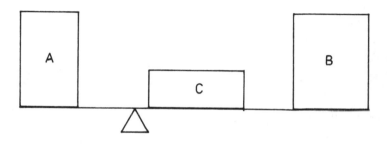

A A
B B
C C

Answer

Q34. Which of these shapes is the hardest to turn over?

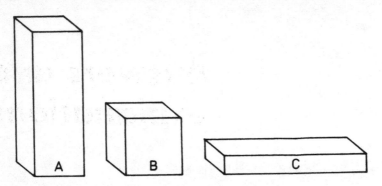

A A
B B
C C

Answer [   ]

10

Answers and explanations

Chapter 6: Technical numerical questions

Section one

Q1. D	Q2. D	Q3. A	Q4. C	Q5. B
Q6. B	Q7. C	Q8. C	Q9. C	Q10. C
Q11. C	Q12. D	Q13. C	Q14. C	Q15. C
Q16. C	Q17. C	Q18. D	Q19. B	Q20. D
Q21. D	Q22. C	Q23. E	Q24. C	Q25. D
Q26. D	Q27. E	Q28. A	Q29. B	Q30. C

Section two

Q1. 9.4	Q2. 266	Q3. 6	Q4. 23
Q5. 3	Q6. 127	Q7. 15.84	Q8. × (multiply)
Q9. 21	Q10. 972	Q11. – (minus)	Q12. 11
Q13. 1,000 g	Q14. 47.6	Q15. 4	Q16. 12
Q17. 10	Q18. 188	Q19. 16.7	Q20. × (multiply)
Q21. 1,016	Q22. 7,112	Q23. 22.5 (approx)	
Q24. 4 (approx)		Q25. 311.6 cm	

Q26. 104.3 cm   Q27. 191.8 cm   Q28. 171 cm
Q29. 148.4 cm   Q30. 1,260 cm

Practice test

Q1. B
Q2. B
Q3. A
Q4. D
Q5. B
Q6. D
Q7. D
Q8. D
Q9. C
Q10. B
Q11. D
Explanation $8 \times 9 = 72; 72 - 15 = 57$

Q12. A
Explanation $212 - 43 = 169; 169 - 9 = 160$

Q13. A
Explanation $7 \times 2.5 = 17.5$ m; 500 cm = 5 m; $17.5 - 5 = 12.5$; ?
+ 300 mm = 12.5 m; 12.5 m − 300 mm = 12.2 m; so ? = 12.2 m

Q14. B
Explanation $40 \div 5 = 8; 73 - 8 = 65$

Q15. D
Explanation $2,000 \times 0.0022 = 4.4$

Q16. B
Explanation $120 \div 3 = 40$

Q17. D
Explanation $15 \times 2.54 = 38.1$

Q18. C
Explanation $5 \times 1,016 = 5,080$

Q19. C
Explanation one million = 1,000,000

Q20. A
Explanation 19 × 4.5 = 85.5

Area, volume and surface areas

Q1. D
Explanation Area of a square = length × breadth; in the case of a square length = breadth.

Q2. C
Explanation 2.5 × 2.5 = 6.25

Q3. D
Explanation 12 × 12 = 144

Q4. D
Explanation A square has four sides of equal length so the perimeter is 12 + 12 + 12 + 12 = 48.

Q5. B
Explanation The rectangle has 4 sides; 2 are 2 cm long and 2 arc 3 cm long so its perimeter = 2 + 2 + 3 + 3 = 10.

Q6. A
Explanation The perimeter of the square is 2 + 2 + 2 + 2 = 8. The perimeter of the rectangle is 8 + 8 + 4 + 4 = 24, but the two shapes share a side so you must deduct one side of the square from the total of each shape. The perimeter = 8 + 24 – 2 – 2 = 28.

Q7. C
Explanation Volume is the space occupied by a three-dimensional shape. The volume of a cube is found by multiplying its length by its breadth by its height. So 2 × 2 × 2 = 8.

Q8. C
Explanation 4 × 4 × 4 = 64

Q9. D
Explanation $6 \times 6 \times 6 = 216$

Q10. D
Explanation In the diagram you can see only 3 sides but think of a dice with sides numbered 1 to 6.

Q11. C
Explanation Each side of the cube has an area of 4 cm^2. The surface area is $4 \times 6 = 24$.

Q12. E
Explanation Each side has an area of 16 cm^2; $16 \times 6 = 96$.

Q13. B

Q14. B
Explanation Volume of a cuboid = length × breadth × height = 6 × 2 × 2 = 24.

Q15. A
Explanation $10 \times 3 \times 4 = 120$

Q16. D
Explanation $11 \times 1 \times 2 = 22$

Q17. C
Explanation The cuboid is made up of two ends each 2 cm × 2 cm, and four lengths each 5 cm × 2 cm.

Q18. B
Explanation The two ends are 2 cm × 3 cm, two of the lengths are 5 cm × 2 cm and the remaining two sides are 5 cm × 3 cm.

Q19. C
Explanation The areas of the surfaces add up as follows: $(2 \times 2) + (2 \times 2) + (5 \times 2) + (5 \times 2) + (5 \times 2) + (5 \times 2) = 48$.

Q20. B
Explanation The cuboid has 3 pairs of identical sides. They are $2 \times (6 \times 2) + 2 \times (6 \times 3) + 2 \times (3 \times 2) = (2 \times 12) + (2 \times 18) + (2 \times 6) = 24 + 36 + 12 = 72$.

Q21. A
Explanation It has three pairs of identical sides: 2 (2.5 × 1) + 2 (8 × 2.5) + 2 (8 × 1) = 5 + 40 + 16 = 61.

Q22. B
Explanation The area of a right-angled triangle is found with ½ × breadth × height = ½ × 4 × 2 = ½ × 8 = 4.

Q23. D
Explanation ½ × 7 × 3 = ½ × 21 = 10.5

Q24. B
Explanation ½ × 4 × 4 = ½ × 16 = 8

Q25. 12.5 cm^2
Explanation Treat the triangle as two right-angled triangles stuck together. Then you can work it out as follows: ½ height × breadth = ½ × 5 × 2.5 = 6.25; 6.25 × 2 = 12.5.

Q26. 21 cm^2
Explanation ½ × 7 × 3 = 10.5; 10.5 × 2 = 21

Q27. 16 cm^2
Explanation ½ × 8 × 2 = 8; 8 × 2 = 16

Trainability and selection tests in construction

Q1. 67.4 m^2
Explanation 6 × 12 = 72 (this is the size of the shaded area including the door). Subtract the area of the door: 2 × 2.3 = 4.6; 72 – 4.6 = 67.4.

Q2. 18 m^2
Explanation ½ × 12 × 3 = 18

Q3. 4.6 m^2
Explanation 2 × 2.3 = 4.6

Q4. 3.37 litres
Explanation Shaded area = 67.4 m^2 ÷ 20 = 3.37.

Q5. 13.5 m^2
Explanation Door = 2.5 × 3 = 7.5. Windows = 1 × 2 = 2; 2 × 3 = 6; 7.5 + 6 = 13.5.

Q6. 15 m^2
Explanation Divide the roof into four identical right-angled triangles: ½ × 2.5 × 3 = 3.75 × 4 = 15.

Q7. 106.5 m^2
Explanation 20 × 6 = 120 – 13.5 = 106.5

Q8. 121.5 m^2
Explanation Shaded area 106.5 + the roof 15 = 121.5.

Q9. 6
Explanation 106.5 ÷ 20 = 5.325, so you would need 6 litre tins.

Q10. 343 m^3
Explanation 7 × 7 × 7 = 343

Q11. 192.25 m^2
Explanation 7 × 7 = 49; 49 × 4 = 196; 196 – (1.5 × 2.5 = 3.75) = 192.25

Q12. 49 m^2
Explanation 7 × 7 = 49

Q13. 19.2 litres
Explanation Remember, two coats; area of walls = 192.25 m^2 ÷ 20 = 9.6 × 2 = 19.2.

Q14. 144 m^3
Explanation 12 × 3 × 4 = 144

Q15. 48 m^2
Explanation 12 × 4 = 48

Q16. 88.55 m^2
Explanation 12 × 3 = 36 × 2 = 72; 4 × 3 = 12 × 2 = 24; 72 + 24 = 96; door = 1.5 × 2.3 = 3.45; window = 2 × 2 = 4; 3.45 + 4 = 7.45; 96 – 7.45 = 88.55

Q17. 1.92 litres
Explanation 4 × 12 = 48 ÷ 25 = 1.92

Electrical power

Exercise 1
Q1. 28	Q2. 54	Q3. 105	Q4. 225	Q5. 550
Q6. 3,250	Q7. 2,880	Q8. 1,430	Q9. 4,500	
Q10. 800				

Exercise 2
Q1. 5	Q2. 5	Q3. 6	Q4. 11.5	Q5. 10
Q6. 10	Q7. 20	Q8. 26	Q9. 15	Q10. 10

Exercise 3
Q1. 5.88	Q2. 6.88	Q3. 100	Q4. 17.45	Q5. 47.50
Q6. 27.50	Q7. 35.63	Q8. 11.85	Q9. 10.31	
Q10. 18.54				

Exercise 4
Q1. 5	Q2. 2	Q3. 4	Q4. 1	Q5. 6
Q6. 3	Q7. 3	Q8. ¼ (0.25)	Q9. ½ (0.5)	Q10. 2

Exercise 5
Q1. 225	Q2. 50	Q3. 192	Q4. 266	Q5. 300
Q6. 425	Q7. 455	Q8. 675	Q9. 9	Q10. 25

Exercise 6
Q1. 450	Q2. 45	Q3. 24	Q4. 150	Q5. 48
Q6. 84	Q7. 54	Q8. 32	Q9. 324	Q10. 24

Exercise 7

Q1. 4	Q2. 6	Q3. 7	Q4. 12	Q5. 24
Q6. 5	Q7. 3	Q8. 14	Q9. 17	Q10. 19
Q11. 24	Q12. 48	Q13. 12	Q14. 16	Q15. 6
Q16. 1	Q17. 96	Q18. 25	Q19. 8	Q20. 15

Exercise 8

Q1. 1.75	Q2. 3	Q3. 8	Q4. 0.5	Q5. 1.5
Q6. 0.75	Q7. 11.5	Q8. 22.50	Q9. 12	Q10. 2
Q11. 17	Q12. 14	Q13. 8.50	Q14. 19.50	
Q15. 24.25	Q16. 7.25	Q17. 12.25	Q18. 19	
Q19. 6.75	Q20. 3.75			

Chapter 7: Technical verbal questions

Basic vocabulary of science and engineering

Q1. C	Q2. C	Q3. A	Q4. D	Q5. B
Q6. A	Q7. C	Q8. B	Q9. B	Q10. C
Q11. D	Q12. A	Q13. E	Q14. E	Q15. C
Q16. D	Q17. A	Q18. C	Q19. B	Q20. C
Q21. D	Q22. C	Q23. A	Q24. C	Q25. B
Q26. A	Q27. E	Q28. C	Q29. A	Q30. F
Q31. C	Q32. C	Q33. E	Q34. A	Q35. A
Q36. C	Q37. D	Q38. E	Q39. C	Q40. A
Q41. C	Q42. B	Q43. E	Q44. D	Q45. C
Q46. C	Q47. A	Q48. D	Q49. B	Q50. D
Q51. A	Q52. B	Q53. B	Q54. D	Q55. B
Q56. A	Q57. A	Q58. E	Q59. B	Q60. C
Q61. B	Q62. E	Q63. A	Q64. C	Q65. A
Q66. B	Q67. A	Q68. A		

Basic principles of physics

Q1. C
Q2. B
Q3. A
Q4. A
Q5. A
Q6. B
Q7. A

Explanation It reflects the light of the sun rather than producing its own visible light.

Q8. B
Q9. B

Explanation The image is laterally inverted.

Q10. C
Q11. D
Q12. A and B
Q13. B
Q14. D, B, C, A, E
Q15. C

Explanation The sound must travel to the object and back so the object is half the distance travelled by the sound wave: $3 \times 340 = 1,020 \div 2 = 510$.

Q16. D

Explanation The boiling point of water will lower with a reduction of atmospheric pressure, so from this you can tell that the answer is either 35 °C or 70 °C.

Q17. B, D, F, G, C, A, E

Explanation The visible colours occur in the spectrum in the descending order of red, orange, yellow, green, blue, indigo and violet (ROYGBIV).

Q18. B
Q19. D, A, B, C

Explanation The battery contains chemical energy, which transfers to electric energy; this becomes kinetic energy when the motor turns and finally remains as potential energy.

Q20. B
Q21. C
Q22. C
Q23. B
Q24. A
Q25. C

Explanation The paint is given the same charge so the particles spread out evenly; the surface being sprayed is given the opposite charge so that it attracts the paint.

Q26. B

Explanation You multiply volume by density to get mass.

Q27. C
Q28. A

Explanation Answer B is the latent heat of fusion.

Q29. C

Explanation Gravity on the Moon is about one-sixth of that on Earth.

Q30. B
Q31. A
Q32. D

Chapter 8: Tests of diagrammatic reasoning

Q1. D	Q2. B	Q3. A	Q4. B	Q5. C
Q6. E	Q7. C	Q8. C	Q9. D	Q10. B
Q11. A	Q12. B	Q13. D	Q14. D	Q15. C
Q16. A	Q17. B	Q18. E	Q19. B	

Chapter 9: Mechanical questions

Section one

Q1. C	Q2. B	Q3. B	Q4. A	Q5. D
Q6. B	Q7. B	Q8. A	Q9. B	Q10. B
Q11. B	Q12. C	Q13. B	Q14. B	Q15. A

Section two

Q16. A	Q17. C	Q18. C	Q19. A	Q20. A
Q21. A	Q22. A	Q23. D	Q24. A	Q25. C
Q26. B	Q27. C	Q28. B	Q29. C	Q30. A
Q31. B	Q32. C	Q33. A	Q34. C	

Further reading from Kogan Page

Books

The Advanced Numeracy Test Workbook, Mike Bryon, 2003

Aptitude, Personality and Motivation Tests: Assess Your Potential and Plan Your Career, 2nd edition, Jim Barrett, 2004

The Aptitude Test Workbook, Jim Barrett, 2003

The Graduate Psychometric Test Workbook, Mike Bryon, 2005

Great Answers to Tough Interview Questions: How to Get the Job You Want, 6th edition, Martin John Yate, 2005

How to Master Personality Questionnaires, 2nd edition, Mark Parkinson, 2000

How to Master Psychometric Tests, 3rd edition, Mark Parkinson, 2004

How to Pass Advanced Aptitude Tests, Jim Barrett, 2002

How to Pass the Civil Service Qualifying Tests, 2nd edition, Mike Bryon, 2003

How to Pass Computer Selection Tests, Sanjay Modha, 1994

How to Pass Firefighter Recruitment Tests, Mike Bryon, 2004

How to Pass Graduate Psychometric Tests, 2nd edition, Mike Bryon, 2001

How to Pass the New Police Selection System, 2nd edition, Harry Tolley, Billy Hodge and Catherine Tolley, 2004

How to Pass Numeracy Tests, 2nd edition, Harry Tolley and Ken Thomas, 2000

How to Pass Numerical Reasoning Tests, Heidi Smith, 2003

How to Pass Professional Level Psychometric Tests, 2nd edition, Sam Al-Jajjoka, 2004

How to Pass Selection Tests, 3rd edition, Mike Bryon and Sanjay Modha, 2005

How to Pass Verbal Reasoning Tests, 2nd edition, Harry Tolley and Ken Thomas, 2000

IQ and Psychometric Test Workbook, Philip Carter, 2005

Preparing Your Own CV: How to Improve Your Chances of Getting the Job You Want, 3rd edition, Rebecca Corfield, 2003

Readymade CVs: Sample CVs for Every Type of Job, 3rd edition, Lynn Williams, 2004

Readymade Job Search Letters: Every Type of Letter for Getting the Job You Want, 3rd edition, Lynn Williams, 2004

Successful Interview Skills, Rebecca Corfield, 1992

Test Your Own Aptitude, 3rd edition, Jim Barrett and Geoff Williams, 2003

The Ultimate Interview Book, Lynn Williams, 2005

CD ROMS

Psychometric Tests, Volume 1, The Times Testing Series, Editor Mike Bryon 2002

Test Your Aptitude, Volume 1, The Times Testing Series, Editor Mike Bryon, 2002

Test Your IQ, Volume 1, The Times Testing Series, Editor Mike Bryon, 2002

The above titles are available from all good bookshops. For further information contact the publisher at the address below:

Kogan Page Limited
120 Pentonville Road
London N1 9JN
United Kingdom
Tel: 020 7278 0433
Fax: 020 7837 6348
Website: www.kogan-page.co.uk